TAKE THE DE-OUT OF DEPRESSION AND PRESS ON!

by Janine A. Alexander M.S.E.

DORRANCE
PUBLISHING CO
EST. 1920
PITTSBURGH, PENNSYLVANIA 15238

The contents of this work, including, but not limited to, the accuracy of events, people, and places depicted; opinions expressed; permission to use previously published materials included; and any advice given or actions advocated are solely the responsibility of the author, who assumes all liability for said work and indemnifies the publisher against any claims stemming from publication of the work.

The cover of this book was design and illustrated by Jarred Elrod, my son-in-law, married to Amanda.

Dorrance Publishing Co
585 Alpha Drive
Suite 103
Pittsburgh, PA 15238
Visit our website at www.dorrancebookstore.com

ISBN: 979-8-8860-4334-1
eISBN: 979-8-8860-4895-7

The friend I spoke of in Chapter De-Serve, has since passed away,
This book is written in part in loving memory of Susan Benson.

This book is written in memory of my parents,
W.J. and JoAnn Alexander,
who raised me with a sense of Judeo-Christian values.

This book is written in honor of my children,
Amanda, Chase, and Autumn,
who have inspired me through many of life events
and the writings of this book.

CONTENTS

Write your own success story...your own Chapter.... Claim it!

Chapter One: DE-AL ...

1. distribute (cards) in an orderly rotation to players for a game or round.

2. take part in commercial trading of a particular commodity.

3. take measures concerning (someone or something), with the intention of putting something right.

4. inflict (a blow) on (someone or something).

Similar: take measure, take action, confront.

DEAL.....Take the De- out and deal with ALL of it.

Many times when faced with decisions to confront a situation, many of us would chose to avoid it rather than confront it. Confrontation has a bad reputation. It doesn't have to be negative. Confront – face up to, deal with, bring something to light, and get it out into the open. **Deal** with it! Take the DE- out and deal, deal with **ALL** of it.

How many times have we sensed the "uncomfortableness" of a situation and let it pass us by only to have it resurface, bigger and badder the next round. Let me use this example. A splinter; a small, tiny piece of wood in your finger. Inflicting so much discomfort, sometimes even really painful. OUCH! Time to get it out.

You attempt to get it with a pair of tweezers and think you have been successful. Weeks pass by and you notice something in the same spot where the splinter was because it has become more uncomfortable. Hummmmm? Resolution: get the tweezers and dig deeper (another chapter) into the flesh. Except now it has formed a callous and it's tougher than it was originally. Well, use more grit. More determination (another chapter.) It's coming out, whether it likes it or not! You're going to end this once and for all. Deal with it!

Can you think of an example in your life where you put off confronting an issue, postponed the inevitable, and your actions resulted in a bigger problem? We all have … We all have fallen short of the glory of God. But he is the God of second chances.

I'm using the story of Jonah here. He was so deep into denial he landed *deep* into a whale's belly! YUCK! Can you imagine how uncomfortable that had to of been. I consider it a life metaphor. When we don't obey our gut, our instincts, or God's instructions, we could very well end up in a worse situation. He didn't want to confront the issue: the people of Ninevah, so God had him eaten upby a big fish. (If you care to read the story, go to the book of Jonah in the Old Testament. It made for a great bible story when I was a kid in vacation bible school. It has a different life application now that I'm an adult.)

How many times have we denied our calling and avoided issues only to find ourselves facing much worse conditions or stress we could have avoided if we had just faced, confronted, or better yet, DEalt with the issue in front of us.

Back to Jonah: "I called out of my trouble and distress to the Lord and he answercd me!" *Jonah 2:2.*

So, what was Jonah's response? 2:6 "You have brought up my life from the pit (death.)And in the end, God demonstrated great compassion. Even toward the people of Ninevah, when they turned from their evil ways. Jonah still didn't get it. H asked God to kill him. In the end, God's compassion won! We may not be caught up in "evil." It might be something as simple as just not listening to the "voice" inside warning us. It could be as simple as not telling a friend your feelings were hurt, so it festers into a spirit of resentment. I related a Bible story, now a real life story.

I was listening to a Podcast on my way home from Orlando with my new friend, Jeanne, who is studying to be a family therapist. She, is a mother of six children, which I assured her qualifies her in many ways. So, "the Crappy Childhood Fairy" relates a story from a letter she received.

Two friends had discussed a trip to Mexico, but hadn't formulated any specific plans. Then, the one friend (one), calls to tell friend (two) her boyfriend and she are going on this trip. You can imagine the feelings that surfaced in friend two. However, rather than express her feelings, she let them fester into feelings of resentment and bitterness. She related how it turned into depression.

So, imagine if she had expressed those feelings and confronted the issue, as her disappointment was obvious, then told the friend "I'm happy for you, but ..." By airing the matter, DE-al-ing with it, rather than letting it formulate harder feelings and internalizing, which prevents further damage to the relationship, causes potential psychological manifestations, and even physical diseases. Dealing with matters as they arise can truly prevent further harm to our psyche and our physiological body. I believe many cancers could be prevented if we tended to our psyche before it manifested into a physical disease.

Suppression, Oppression, and repression leads to ... depression. This is often true of traumatic events which can resurface as post-traumatic stress disorder (PTSD.) I mentioned in a later chapter a rape when I was a college freshman which I hid (suppressed) for10-years. The treatments I have received were from two very skilled and qualified therapists who are well-known for treating PTSD and CPTSD. I will expand on these modalities in another chapter.

EMDR: (Eye movement desensitization and reprocessing), founded by Francine Shapiro, in 1987.

ART: Accelerated Resolution Therapy, developed by Laney Rosenzweig in 2008.

Please don't let the fear of what you might discover keep you from the freedom healing brings! Deal with it! ALL of it! Get that splinter out! If we De- all, with it when it happens, we are far more likely to heal more quickly without the residual damage of becoming calloused or bitter. I want to encourage you today! Dig deep. Find that wound which may have developed from childhood or adulthood, and **Deal with it.** Don't waste another day cycling the negative emotions. Let forgiveness flow from your heart! Open yourself up to the possibilities of life without pain and suffering.

For his anger is but for a moment, and his favor is for a lifetime. Joy comes in the morning! Psalms 30: 1-5.

Take the DE- out of deal and, **DEAL with** all of it!

Chapter Two: DE-BILITATING

1) making someone very weak and infirm.
2) tending to weaken something.
Similar: weakening, enfeebling, enervating, devitalizing, draining, de-energizing, sapping wearing, exhausting, tiring, impairing, crippling, paralyzing

Statistically over 1 million people in the United States suffer from depression as of a 2019 census. That's one too many!

Scenario:
It's a beautiful, sunny, 70-degree day outside, but you are buried under the covers, unable to stir the desire to get out of bed. The voices in your mind say your worthless, stupid, unmotivated, and incapable of change. Your whole body aches and is filled with potato-sack like fatigue. No one in this world cares you are in the condition you're in and they're not there to encourage you out of it. Your can't think of a reason to continue with this life, as you consider yourself a waste of space and energy.

That's often the mindset of a depressed person ... it's debilitating. This is an accurate description coming from the author of this book – me. Oh, I forgot the final blow. This world would be a better place without me ... Woe is me!

When I finally do arouse myself, the gravel doesn't seem to clear from my view. It's a haze that lingers all day, causing lack of clarity, thought, and confusion. I have difficulty making decisions, a lack of confidence, and a chronic, unexplainable fatigue. I commonly suffered from gross body aches and pains, from headaches to muscular tension. When was enough, enough? I fought through it for months. It's not unusual to have some down moods following certain life events, such as a loss of job, death of family members or friends, or an unexpected medical diagnosis. I'm sure you can think of a situation where the fog hung around a little too long. If you are questioning whether or not you have suffered from or currently suffer from a form of depression, I want to encourage you to take action, medical advice, and treatment. As is key with any disease, albeit physical or psychological, prompt proper diagnosis and treatment can help remediate the symptoms and potential reoccurrence.

Here we go again! I'm Being vulnerable and transparent so my reading audience understands, I really do understand! How many of us have had someone say, "I understand," while we are staring them in the face, knowing they could not possibly understand. This became apparent to me one time when I was trying to explain to someone who clearly did not understand. The comment "I understand" is quite dismissive, if there is no understanding. It totally lacks empathy; that feeling of being in someone else's shoes ... So, I developed this response instead, "I couldn't begin to understand the feelings or heartache you are experiencing, but I am here for you if you need to talk, and I will pray for you and support you through this as your friend." This response can open the door for empathy, understanding, and further conversations to what is happening and what might need to be addressed immediately!

These writings come from my heart, from a place of healing, but also from a place of sorrow. For those who know the impact mental illness as severe depression has led many a desperate soul to end their own lives while in such a dark place they couldn't see their way out! I've been there; in that dark place. Please read on ...

Buried beneath the covers on a beautifully sunny day, without explanation for how I was feeling, but I knew my heart was weak, yet heavy. So deeply sorrowful my whole body hurt. To someone experiencing this level of depression, it's hard to imagine it will ever subside.

David speaks to this level of emotional torment in the Psalms 109.

Verse 22: "For I am suffering and needy, and my heart is wounded within me. I am vanishing like a shadow when it lengthens and fades; I am shaken off like the locust. My knees are unsteady from fasting; And my flesh is gaunt and without fatness. I also have become a reproach and an object of taunting to others. When they see me they shake their heads [in derision]." (Matt. 26;39) This is taken from the Everyday Life Bible, Amplified version, distributed through Joyce Meyer Ministries.

David is so depressed, even his physical body is manifesting the symptoms of disease. I understand …

Some of the Symptoms of Depression are listed in another chapter, but let's revisit them here.

- Foggy thinking
- Confusion
- Difficulty making decisions
- Fatigue
- Headaches
- Sleeping too much
- Sleeplessness
- Ruminating thoughts
- Tearfulness
- Low mood

I was in my health classroom, teaching the mental health unit, going over a check list with my students. I checked every one of the symptoms. I advised my students to see the counselor if they had any concerns, but one of my students came to me and explained she had been involved in a car accident, which brought on depression and anxiety, and was on Zoloft, which didn't seem to be working. I advised her to consult with her physician to regulate the dosage.

Please don't let debilitating depression keep you from acting on your own health needs! Consult with a trusted friend or family member and set an action plan into motion!

Take the de- out of Debilitating and start your rehabilitation today!

Habilitate - To make fit or capable.

When a person struggles with depression, much of their innate drive or desire is impacted negatively. Their "get up and go" has got up and left! I dealt with this debilitating depression for years. But one thing I cling to is, GET STARTED! Find something productive to feed your productivity daily. Even the smallest tasks, or feats, can rebuild desire and confidence, and boost your mood!

May I share the things I do for myself that are self-care essentials to combat depression? First, I believe there is a strong spiritual connection. We are at war with our negative thoughts. Author and speaker, Joyce Meyer, has written a book called *Battlefield of the MIND*, which is very insightful. Joel Osteen speaks of "Daily Affirmations" to replace negative thoughts with positive ones. Rick Warren has written the book, *Purpose Driven Life*. Start your day (even while still in bed) with thoughts of good things. Stretch! Breathe! Come alive. Get a plan mapped out. Your day does not have to be filled with activity. Anything you do to be proactive can aid in your recovery.

Allow yourself some down time. If you have a regular job with regular hours, take some time during your day for a walk and break. Re-charge! I over-stressed myself for years thinking more was better. If I could pack 15 things to do in a day, I would. However, inevitably, I wouldn't get them all done, which fed the defeated mentality. Prioritize the things which need your attention first. If you work, your job needs your energy. If you have family, you must devote some time and energy for them. If you have a spouse, by all means do not neglect that relationship. Other tasks and things are less significant and less meaningful than close relationships.

When I was teaching, I was also coaching and running a 15-hour day! I was constantly running myself in overdrive. As a mother of three and a wife, I am sure everyone in my path was neglected to some degree, including myself. By the time I recognized I had multiple symptoms, I was clinically depressed. I truly believe this contributed to my brain's low serotonin levels, which can contribute to depression. The brain is a very sensitive organ with many neurotransmitters and neuropathways. I compare it to a car with 12-cylinders, and when depressed is only firing on six or eight. The rhythm is off. The timing is off. Every mechanism under the hood suffers.

I developed a sleep disorder after my third child, waking up every two hours like clockwork. I wasn't sure if the sleep deprivation was impacting the depression, or if depression was causing sleep deprivation. It's taken several years to get my sleep regulated, with the occasional aid of medications, melatonin, and Benadryl (Diphenhydramine), on a rotation as needed. Sometimes medication is absolutely necessary, and only your trusted health care professional should assess, diagnose and prescribe. I have personal experience with medication and other "natural" remedies. It is truly a trial and error process with the brain. What works for one person may not work for you. I was willing to explore my options and I recommend you keep an open mind to what your options are.

Exercise - I have a master's degree in Exercise Physiology, and I believe wholeheartedly in the benefits of exercise for fitness, to alleviate stress, and for more conducive sleep. Plus, the benefits to your physical appearance help with your self-image and confidence.

Aerobic exercise has been proven to elevate brain chemicals called endorphins for periods of four hours post-exercise. Aerobic exercise comes in the form of a rhythmic activity like walking, swimming, running, cycling, etc., which increases the body's demand for oxygen. It elevates oxygen in your blood and brain! Learn to breathe more deeply while exercising and at rest.

De-Stress - Reduce your expectations for a time, where you accomplish your daily goals in a reasonable manner. Learn to say "no" to other tasks which are going to add to your stress. Yes, others will not like hearing "no," but your mind and body will begin to respond to the reduction in work load.

One thing I wasn't going to do was to compromise my exercise schedule, the one thing that I could count on alleviating depression.

Relaxation techniques - these come in many forms – yoga, long walks, deep slow breathing, meditation, and even an occasional massage. Some of these may cost you, but if you allow for space in your budget, you'll realize the benefits far outweigh the costs.

Re-habilitation can be a long process. It can be a life-long process. Taking the de- out of depression and pressing on means finding that place inside yourself only you know, and with God's help, you can resolve what caused the onset and perpetuated the problem. It means digging DEEP; Having an epiphany, facing some uncomfortableness, and asking yourself, "how much do I desire a healing?"

I believe healing is a process, as well, and when we stay in a mindset of healing, it will come – a moment, day, week, and year at a time!

Referring back to Psalms 109, Verse 26: "Help me, O LORD, my GOD! Save me according to your loving-kindness. And let me know that this is your hand. I have great praise and thanks to the LORD with my mouth. And in the midst of many, I will praise him." David's spirit is lifted! Remember this is the same David we spoke of earlier who was depressed! David is using positive affirmations and acknowledging "GOD's hand" in the process. I believe GOD is the GREAT healer, but he also puts skilled, trained, and qualified professionals in our lives to assist in the process.

Don't delay any further! Don't lose another moment, day, week, or year to depression. take the DE-out of depression and PRESS ON!

These two Scriptures speak to "pressing on": Ecclesiastes 9:11 r "Let us know that the race is not to the swift, nor the battle to the strong, but _to the one_ who _holds out._"

God wants us to keep on striving, keep on trying, and keep moving on, trying to reach our goal. Never give up! So, first of all, we must stay focused, and secondly, we must _press on._

Philippians 3: 13 -14 (NIV) 13. "I count not myself to have apprehended but this one thing I do, forgetting those things which are behind, and reaching forth unto those things which are before [...] I <u>press</u> toward the mark of the prize of the high calling of GOD in Christ Jesus."

I suggest you pick one and meditate on it daily, set a goal and find your purpose, hold out for a miracle. Hold out for a Healing!

Take the De-out of De-habilitated and rehabilitate yourself to be fit and capable for living a more joyful, productive life.

Chapter Three: DE-BUNK

expose the falseness or hollowness of (a myth, idea, or belief).
"the magazine that debunks claims of the paranormal"
Similar: explode, deflate, puncture, quash, knock the bottom out
of, expose

There's a myth that Depression is a Mental health condition that often *requires* medication.

So, when I initially went to be evaluated by the psychiatrist that my former employer referred me to, he asked if I had ever considered taking an anti-depressant. So, I was willing to try whatever he recommended, and psychotherapy. Just feeling like someone else cared and understood, was enough to give me an initial boost. In all of my years of treatment, no one offered that Depression had more than a physiological, brain chemical origin, or triggered by my thoughts from life events.

Has anyone ever asked: "is there something in your spiritual life that needs to be explored". Yes, spiritual being the operative word. Humans are composed of a mind, body, and spirit. The body contains all of the metabolic, physiological and neurological functions and organs, The mind and spirit, however, can overpower all of these......can I will myself into a better mood? Yes, I do it daily.......I can change my thoughts processes on a moment's notice. If you can decline to believe a thought, you can change the course of Depression. I have often heard it said, What the mind can conceive the body can achieve.

With the renewing of our minds, we can overcome disease, physiological and psychological. Our thoughts are just that powerful.

You can lower your blood pressure, by breathing and taking yourself to a friendly place, in a period of stress which could have an adverse impact. I've done it.......

I believe Depression, can be reduced by identifying the events, or times in our lives that have left us feeling downhearted, in despair, defeated, devalued, demeaned, demoralized, ...you see the pattern?

Anything that may have impacted us spiritually and left us Devoid of enough emotional strength or integrity to "deal" with it at the time. Once we identify the source or the root of the issue and go to work on eliminating the "bunk" that was created by situation.

Let me use the example of an experience with Sexual assault. Many victims of such, tend to blame themselves. They fault themselves, as if they did something to deserve this kind of treatment, and don't report it. By carrying the burden, reverting into a state of denial, they subject themselves to long-term psychological harm.

I can speak to this, having been the victim of a date-rape in college. I carried the burden for 10 years, and when I finally revealed the event to my therapist, I learned that by putting the blame on the perpetrator and then forgiving myself, I initiated the healing process. By De- bunking my own thoughts that I was at fault, I put the blame on the appropriate party, the perpetrator. Often, we own fault we shouldn't. I've learned to own my part, but not to take on the part of the other person if someone else is involved.

Get rid of the myth, the idea, or Belief, if it is false, the fault, the burden of blame.......forgive yourself, and others. It's a form of early intervention to avoid Depression that could come from carrying long term guilt or shame.

These are some applicable scriptures.

Cast all your cares on him, for he cares for you. *1 Peter 5:7*

Cast your cares on the LORD and he will sustain you: he will never let the righteous be shaken. *Psalms 55:22*

I grew up hearing the comment, "Shame on you". So I ask, why would we want to impute shame on anyone that is attempting to live a Godly life. We all have fallen short of his glory, but his grace is sufficient.

Let's take the De- out of Debunk, Get rid of the "bunk" in our lives and live in his truth. That we are truly "fearfully and wonderfully" made, *Psalms 139.* and that his mercy endures forever, Oh, Give thanks unto the L ORD, His mercy endures forever, *Psalms 136.*

And *John 8:31-32:* The truth will set you free, If you abide in my word, you are truly my disciples, and you will know the truth, and the "truth will set you free".

Chapter Four: DE-BRIEF

a series of questions about a completed mission or undertaking. Similar: question, quiz, interview, examine, cross-examine, interrogate

Initially, this chapter was going to be my last......because it was the happy ending to your story on depression. Keeping it brief. But when suggested to alphabetize it just made sense from an organizational perspective. If you prefer, you may skip and reserve this chapter until "The END". Happy endings are always preferred! The JOY of the LORD is my Strength. When Christ died at calvary, it is said, "It is finished". Let's keep this brief......let this book encourage you to end your war with Depression by claiming the victory! Every day, every hour, every minute, live life more abundantly.

Take the De-out of Depression and PRESS ON! toward the prize of the high calling.

He called us to live life abundantly and victoriously.

It is my hope that this book guides you to life giving water, the water in his word.

It is my prayer that you be healed and come out of the Darkness and into the LIGHT!

It is God's desire that you find the life he intended for us to live on this planet, while we are here for such a short time, considering his eternal promises!

I'll be Brief........ in God's name AMEN!

The LORD's prayer, Our father who art in heaven hollowed be thy name,

The kingdom comes, they will be done ....On earth as it is in heaven.

Finish this .... Give us this day our daily bread, and forgive us our trespasses (sins) as we forgive those who trespass (sin) against us. Lead us not into temptation, but DE-liver us from evil. For thine is the kingdom, the power and the glory, forever and ever.

was going through a divorce with the promise he would be single soon. I was single and available. He was not. Big RED flag! RUN! Someone going through a divorce has not resolved all of the emotions and experiences tied to divorce, ending a marriage. There needs to be a time for healing and reestablishing priorities in a relationship. Nonetheless, we began dating. There were ongoing signs of insecurity and jealousy.

He proposed marriage the same month his divorce was final. I declined as I knew he was on the "rebound." Eventually we separated when it was discovered he was prospecting other women and he became verbally abusive; never a good sign for future fidelity. I say this to say this, if they cheat on their spouse, they will cheat on you. We ended up in a domestic event that would change my life forever. I allowed myself to believe something that wasn't true. He was not available emotionally, and spiritually we were on a different path. We were on a path of deception. How do you prevent deception from happening? I've learned to turn to the LORD when my decisions were in question. I can quote scripture after scripture to support how deception works.

John 8:31-32, "If you abide in my word, you are truly my disciples, and you will know the truth, and the truth will set you free."

"The thief comes only to steal, kill, and destroy. I have come that they may have life and have it more abundantly." *John 10:10*

I'm saying, call it for what it is. When faced with those hard decisions, pray first. God will guide you when we allow him to be a part of our decision-making. When the red flag waves, we can't afford to go into denial. We can't afford to let ourselves be deceived or deceive ourselves into believing other than what we see and know to be true! It's costly. It costs us and our family, it costs us emotionally, spiritually, and physically.

I let being alone, and lonely, skew my judgment. I made it something other than what it was. *I deceived myself into believing it was okay … it wasn't.*

The apostle Paul explains this in, *1 Corinthians 6:18*. He says, "Flee from sexual immorality. Every sin, whatever if a man might do, is outside the body, but the one sinning sexually, sins against the own body."

Sex is the highest form of intimacy humans experience amongst themselves. Participating in the act outside of marriage is like eating the forbidden fruit in the garden. The first bite might taste sweet, but the consequences are far-reaching. So if we succumb to these temptations, what to do then? Repent and ask for forgiveness. "Blessed is the man (woman) that walks not in the counsel of the ungodly, nor stands in the way of sinners, nor sits in the seat of the scornful. But his **delight** is in the law of the Lord; and in his law does he mediate days and night. And he shall be like a tree planted by the rivers of water, that brings forth his fruit in his season; his leaf also shall not wither; and whatsoever he does shall prosper." *Psalms 1: 1-3*

This is coming from a man who knows the personal consequence of his sin – David. I'm always amazed at where God leads me in my writings.

NOTES:
I want to follow this chapter with one on De-lighting in the Lord. When we live in truth, we delight in the LORD. It is a delight to live in truth. The truth will set us free. We can live in the "light." It "light"-ens our load. Be a light unto my path ... DE- Feat

Chapter Six: DE-CLARATION

1. the act of declaring; announcement:
a declaration of a dividend.
2. a positive, explicit, or formal statement; proclamation:
a declaration of war.
something that is announced, avowed, or proclaimed

When I started writing this book, years ago, I was in a similar mindset, but in a totally different place in time. I'm trying to recover this chapter without losing the foundational concept. DECLARE! or Declaration. The process of announcing, avowing, or proclaiming!

In my chapter on Define, take the De-out of define and you'll be fine. Don't let others define who you are, be who you are by GOD's design. I have truly attempted to limit the number of chapters to a "reasonable" amount, and then it came to me – I think it's the holy spirit talking. GOD is not limiting you, so don't limit him.

Definition 2: a positive, explicit, or formal statement; a proclamation. The example given is a **declaration** of war.

If you're an American, or not, most of us were taught about the Declaration of Independence. The Declaration was preempted by a civil war to get to the point of constructing this well-known document, which "declared" our freedom from our mother country. The Declaration of Independence states three basic ideas:

(1) <u>God</u> made all men equal and gave them the rights of life, liberty, and the pursuit of happiness; (2) the main business of government is to protect these rights; (3) if a government tries to withhold these rights, the people are free to revolt and to set up a new government. This is a mini history lesson before we get into our own Declaration of Independence, or Dependence. Let's apply this principle to declaring our freedom from depression. Let me approach making a declaration from this perspective.

If you want to be healed from something, start by declaring a war on it. Begin your fight on depression by declaring a war on it!

2 Chronicles 20:15 And he said, "Hearken ye, all Judah and ye inhabitants of Jerusalem, and thou King Jehoshaphat! Thus saith the LORD unto you: 'Be not afraid nor dismayed by reason of this great multitude; for the battle is not yours, but God's.

Allow me to set the stage for this scripture, though I encourage you to read the whole story for yourself. Solomon, son of David, asked for wisdom in Verse 1 so he could "administer justice to this great people of Yours." GOD granted Solomon wisdom. But wait, there is more! In Verse 12, "I will give you riches, possessions and honor, such as none of the kings who were before you has possessed nor will those who will come after you."

Solomon is not the only person GOD has promised to give wisdom to. He has promised to give wisdom to those who ask. GOD promised to give us the *desires* of our heart. But what happens when all of this gets detoured or derailed by depression? We must rest in his promises …

In the process of researching "the battle is mine" I was detoured by what preceded the battles of Jehoshaphat and found Solomon preceded him. So, I wanted to include what God had done by and through Solomon. We have access to the same promises. We have access to GOD's wisdom and guidance. He is the same GOD of our forefathers. Jehoshaphat was being attacked from all sides by the -ites – Moabites, Ammonites, and Menuites, other places in the Old Testament were other -ites. Historically speaking, there have always been those who would attack, whether man or by spirit or by disease. An attack upon our human being can invoke fear, but instead of fear, God tells us to be of "sound mind." When we "feel" depressed, we can declare we are going to wage war, take on the enemy who wants to rob us of our daily energy, joy, productivity, and relationships. This is what Jehoshaphat did by taking on the enemy.

Ultimately, Jehoshaphat *de*termined he needed to seek GOD and hear from him. He declared, "O LORD....are you not GOD in heaven? You rule over all the kingdoms of the nations? Power and might are in Your hand, there is no one (I add, no spirit, nothing) able to take a stand against YOU!"

This is an acknowledgment. A DECLARATION!

When we can cast our care upon him, and wait for his instruction, we can proceed confidently in our pursuit of a healing, in our battle with the enemy, and dispense of the doubts. We can rely on the GOD of our predecessors, whether characters in the bible or historical figures who had a foundation of faith. We can rely on his word and his promises. We can declare war on the enemies in life who want to steal, kill, and destroy. We can overcome the depression that wants to set us back, keep us down, and live one day at a time, better than the one before.

Together, we can DECLARE a war, and proclaim a victory over depression. We can take the De- out of Depression and Press on toward the prize. Many people describe their fights against cancer or other illnesses as "battling cancer," or "fighting the flu," or "feeling sick." In order to overcome periods of very low mood, I had to take on the battle. One battle at a time!

I armed myself with the necessary weapons to "declare my war." It may sound a bit aggressive, but by the time I realized I was deeply depressed, I believe I was clinically depressed by the symptoms I was experiencing and the length of time I had been experiencing them. I was in crisis mode and contemplating hospitalization. I was in a full-blown depressive episode.

These are the steps I took to seek treatment:

1. I "Declared" I was depressed to myself. The first step was that of self-awareness, acknowledgment, and my symptoms. I admitted I needed

help for what I was experiencing. As is the case with many mental health issues, there is a stigma attached.

2. Initial treatment: I sought help from my internal medicine physician who prescribed Prozac, but made no recommendation for therapy, counseling, or any other activities to accompany the medication. Many times, medications have to be monitored closely as there can be side effects. This was the case with Prozac, I was having side effects. So, I decided to ask for a psychiatric evaluation and was referred to a psychiatric physician. Just as other physicians are specialist, a psychiatrist specializes in the neuroscience of the brain.

3. In addition to medication, I began counseling, "talk therapy," with a licensed mental health counselor. At the time, I was teaching high school and was being sexually harassed by my principal and wasn't able to share with anyone in my environment or at home with my spouse. The feelings of isolation were lifted when I found a caring therapist who allowed me to talk through many of the concerns and issues I was facing at the time. My therapist was knowledgeable and recommended I transfer to another school, which I ultimately did. I continued in my treatment plan for years.

4. Daily exercise: As I have a degree in Exercise Physiology, it has always been a priority and foundation to my physical health but became even more of a priority as I realized the additional benefits to my mental health. Daily exercise. Exercise doesn't have to be extreme. It can be as simple walk around the block to increase breathing, get fresh air, and think positive thoughts. Move your body, change your mind! Find an activity that brings enjoyment to your life. Declare you want your health back – mental, physical, and spiritual health. I recommend a total body, mind, and spirit approach.

5. Manage your nutrition. You notice I don't use the word "diet." Diet usually implies You're going to deprive yourself of something. Monitoring your nutrition implies you're in charge of your daily nutritional plan. Nourish your body and your brain. There is a greater awareness of the benefits of certain nutrients to improve brain function than ever

before. Explore your options in this area. There are certain chemicals which support brain function, such as Omega-oils. I don't have the time or space to go into all of this area in this book. Seek out good advice and educate yourself, then apply the information. Declare you're going to win the battle against things which rob you of nutrition, such as processed foods, simple sugar, and preservatives. You *can* make the changes necessary to nourish your body and fuel your brain to ward off depression.

6. In everything you do, declare you are going to prevail in your pursuit of happiness. Turn what would be seemingly negative into a positive. I've learned, and I'm still learning, the process of overcoming depression. Some days are just better than others. Some days are higher, some days are lower. I try to seek balance and view things more objectively and less subjectively. Moods can change with the weather, but true commitment to better mental health is commitment to living in the moment and bettering each moment.

Even as I write this, I'm having "one of those days" where I ask myself. Do I believe this?

Yes, I believe. Tears flow.

I believe some things are just hard on our hearts and minds, but if we have a firm spiritual foundation and believe in GOD's plan for our life, we will come out of the wilderness and into a promise land, eventually. Again, there's history of this in the Israelites journey through the wilderness to the promised land. Our mood, our emotions, can be managed, and better when not based on outside occurrences or stimuli, other people's opinions or attitudes.

I started listening to podcasts during the 2020 Pandemic and stumbled across one this morning featuring actor Richard Dreyfus. He describes the "darkness" of depression, and stepping out on a bridge you can't see to begin the journey of healing ... stepping out in faith. Reaching out for help from professionals, albeit doctors, psychiatrists, psychologists, therapists, and other mental health advocates and professionals, church programs such as Celebrate Recovery, or other 12-step groups, any or all deserve researching. You have to want it and DECLARE it. Whether you say it out loud or just an internal comment, Declare it.

David said it. Psalms 23, *The LORD is my Shepherd. I shall not want.*

Many times this scripture is referenced at funerals. Today, I want to use it to encourage you! To apply it as an affirmation, as a declaration, to ward off depression.

He is my Shepherd; he has my best interest at heart – to feed, to guide, and to shield me.

I shall not want; when my needs are met.

He lets me lie down in green pastures; he encourages me to rest – body, mind, and spirit.

He leads me beside the still and quiet waters; he calms me. (I swim to reduce stress.)

He refreshes and restores my soul; he renews my mind upon awakening daily.

He leads me in paths of righteousness; knowing we are doing right and is a positive reinforcement. It just makes us feel good. *For his name sake;* We represent well.

Even though I walk through the valley of the shadow of death; this describes the darkness which depression brings. *I will fear no evil for you are with me;* Calm reassurance he has not left our side and will be there through this.

Your rod (protects) *and staff* (guides), *they comfort and console.*

A shepherd uses the tools of his trade to do his job. God has left us the Bible, sent his son, and the HOLY spirit. References which include DECLARE:

Psalms 58, "cry aloud, do not hold back; lift up your voice like a trumpet and *DECLARE...*"

1 John 5:4, for everyone born of God overcomes the world. This is the victory that has overcome the world, *even our faith.*

Deuteronomy 20:4, For the LORD your God is the one who goes with you to *fight for you* against your enemies to give to victory.

Chapter Seven: DE-CLUTTER

remove unnecessary items from (an untidy or overcrowded place).

By now, you are probably asking yourself, "where did she get the words for titles to her chapters? That's a fair question. Some were just very obviously associated to the Book concept, Take the DE- out of Depression and Press ON! Others were developed out of personal experiences, some out of experiences of other people, and still others like this one, are just practical or common sense. Let's see where this goes. Read on.

Scenario: It's raining heavily here with thunder clouds overhead and lightening in the area. I had to forgo my swim! A perfect day for inside activities.

It's March. A perfect month for "Spring cleaning". Hence the title De-clutter.

It goes beyond the surface dust, the superficial things that we might need to clear out of our lives, the lingering junk mail to throw away, or the shelves that need dusting. This is about the deep cleaning, the getting rid of the accumulation of stuff that isn't functional or bringing joy to our lives, the clutter. Many times these are the things that keep us distracted, preventing us from reaching life goals. The CLUTTER.

This could be about the material or immaterial that weighs us down, bogs us down, or clutters our thinking so that clarity we seek isn't so easily accomplished.

Generally, clutter involves things out of our past that have accumulated to a point that it impacts our ability to see a clear path in our futures.

Some people are just naturally more inclined to clutter in their homes, and in their lives. We don't need to look at the why's and wherefores, but it could be beneficial to ask yourself, am I hanging onto something that is weighing me down? Keeping me from experiencing Joy in my life.

Let's use the old pair of shoes in the closet......I'm preparing to do some of this spring cleaning myself, so this is one of my nemesis. SHOES! They are serving a purpose, I can justify keeping them because, my foot size hasn't changed, so I haven't "out grown" them. We can always justify keeping anything in our lives, if we want to.... the questions "Do we need to"? I have to be transparent here, or this writing is of no effect.

The scripture says, Cast of all weights......to run the race! Hebrews 12:1

Some years ago I streamlined my life by getting rid of half my wardrobe, I lightened my load. I can tell you now, that I don't recall half of what I got rid of, but I felt "lighter" and

less encumbered, immediately!

Clutter in our minds can keep us from seeing what is really important to us. Clutter can keep us stuck emotionally. If we deal with the clutter, we can see things more clearly and rid ourselves of emotional baggage that might be weighing us down.

Only you or I can identify those things that are cluttering our lives as they are usually the "shoes" that fit us and we've gotten comfortable with them, thought many times they have holes in the soles...... What about the clutter that creates a hole in our soul? Each of us could identify things that are doing exactly this.... past sins, hidden secrets, labels that we've worn our whole lives, past relationships that were unhealthy or toxic, ...the list goes on.

The scripture puts it like this: in Hebrews **12** Therefore, since we are surrounded by such a great cloud of witnesses, let us throw off everything that hinders and the sin that so easily entangles. And let us run with perseverance the race marked out for us,

You see, the clutter keeps us from being as efficient, and productive, as running our life race, needs not be hindered by things that don't add joy! Un dealt sin that entangles and clutters our minds which could be free from guilt or shame.

Many guilt, shame, and unforgiveness that has cluttered our lives, weighs us down, and creates a heavy heart......which leads to mental and physical depression. That heaviness that accompanies depression, can be dealt with by identifying those areas and "dealing" with them....Refer again to the chapter about taking the DE-out of Deal and deal with all of it! That's where forgiveness of us and others comes in.

Forgive us our debts (sins) as we forgive our debtors (those who sin against us) .....this part of the Lord's prayer addresses unforgiveness and what to do about it. Forgive.

I hope that by aspiring to live a "clutter" free life, we all can run the race that is set for us! The good race!

Galatians 5:7 speaks to this, "You were **run**ning a **good race.** Who cut in on you to keep you from obeying **the** truth? You might take time to read the whole chapter, starting with 5:1, "It is for freedom that Christ has set us free. Stand firm, then, and do not let yourselves be burdened again by a yoke of slavery." Freedom from clutter?

Whether you determine today or in the future to run a better race or live a more clutter free life......it will benefit you in the "long run", and lighten your load.

This might seem funny but, I'm ready to go clean out that closet that I've been procrastinating about!

Take the DE- out of De-clutter and rid yourself of the clutter in your life!

Don't wait! Start running a better race today, one step at a time!

Highly recommended: Joel Osteen podcast on UNCLUTTER Your Mind.

Chapter Eight: DE-EEEP! DEEP DIVE!

1. Extending far down from the top or surface.
2. very intense or extreme.

Epiphany: A manifestation of a divine or supernatural being

I lie awake realizing that the spirit is moving me with ideas on how to begin this chapter..... when an Epiphany occurs. an "aha" moment, a revelation. Those moments of revelation can come from deep within our spirit. The approach I want to take in this chapter is more about digging DEEEEEP! Getting into your spirit where wounds might still exist. These hurts, habits, or hang ups (taken from Celebrate Discovery) can plant deep roots and embed themselves, to the point of making it even more difficult to heal. But healing is always possible, when the desire is there to light the fire!

Let me use this example of digging deep!

Have you ever gotten a splinter in your finger? Then you know how painful that little speck of wood is to your nerve endings! You dig and think you got it all. Relief! Then weeks later you notice the pain has returned.... and maybe even worse a callous has formed, to make it even tougher to get the rest of the splinter out.

Are you getting the picture?

Many times we ignore the "splinters" of old hurts or wounds, and they grow into something worse. The remedy? Dig deeper! Get to the source of the issue, the hurt, the wound, the emotional trauma.....whatever could be standing in the way of a complete healing. The "splinter" could be unforgiveness? Bitterness? Fault-finding? Jealousy? Only you can determine what that splinter is and how deep you need to go to get it all out. As long as the "splinter" is there, the wound can't heal properly......

This is a non-judgment Zone. "Therefore, there is now no condemnation for those who are in Christ Jesus." NIV Romans 8:1

The New King James Version, "Therefore, there is <u>no condemnation</u>, to those who are in Christ Jesus, who do not walk according to the flesh, but according to the Spirit." and Amplified Bible (Joyce Meyer's The Everyday Life Bible)" Therefore there is no condemnation (no guilty verdict, no punishment) for those who are in Christ Jesus."

Digging deep, means finding the EP-iphany the "aha" moment, when this revelation of truth frees us and enlightens us and gives us the JOY of the Lord.

Digging deep, means finding the Strength, and confidence that you are his and he will never leave you or forsake you, even when life gets you down. He picks you up! The JOY of the LORD is our Strength!

Take the De-ep and have the spiritual awakening that is found in his word daily! Dig Deeper every day to find your place of contentment, joy, and healing from Depression.

Chapter Nine: DE-FEATED

1) Win a victory over (someone or something) in a battle or other contest;
2) Overcome or beat
Similar: loss, beating, conquest, conquering. besting, worsting

I'm taking a couple of approaches to this chapter.

1. Coming from the perspective from someone feeling defeated and depressed.
2. Coming from the perspective of someone who has overcome depression.

FEELings of DE-FEAT

The spirit of depression wants to keep us feeling defeated, and it can only do that when we give it permission to do so! Letting <u>strongholds</u> (2 Corinthians 10:4-5) take root in our lives gives way to feeling defeated and depression. I ask myself this one question: Who is in the driver's seat?

God has given us a free will. That means we get to choose, on a daily basis, who we will serve, what we will eat, where we will live, what we will do for a living, and everything we do! We get to choose!

Choose this day to serve him and all these things will be added unto you!

The enemy comes to "steal, kill, and destroy." If the enemy, or in this case, the evil-spirit of depression, can keep us down, then we can't do the work GOD has for us. We can't accomplish his purpose for our lives. Another suggested reading is Rick Warren's book, *A Purpose Driven Life.*

We were meant to live victorious lives.

I'll draw again from Psalms and David's writings. Psalms 42, "As a deer pants for water, so my soul pants (knowingly) for God." David struggled with the enemy, sometimes a physical enemy and sometimes a spiritual enemy! The bouts of depression and his sufferings were obvious. But then, so were the times when he was praising God!

Overcoming DE-feat

Take the DE-out of DEfeat and accomplish the FEAT victoriously.

From the time I was a 13-year-old girl until even into my fifties, I participated in athletic events. I was on sports teams which had a record of winning, but we also had our share of defeats. Whenever we 'lost," we would look back on our performance, correct the mistakes we made, and look forward to a better game or race the next time. Life is full of events; "races" we run and other performance related practices. We can turn anything into a performance. Just because the outcome may not seem in our favor doesn't mean it's a defeat.

A "FEAT" is an achievement which requires great courage, skill, or strength. Even to make an attempt is a success. Many people won't even try for fear of failure. This book is the by-product of overcoming fear. It's a feat which is requiring me to have courage to be transparent and vulnerable. Skill in writing, as I am more of a creative writer and have to rely on outside resources for statistics, and other writers who have gone before me, and the Bible as the sovereign word of God.

Many things require taking risks. With great risks come even greater rewards! The concept of this book is based on running the race! Without the attempt there is no opportunity for victory, for winning, for defeating this thing we call depression.

Just writing this book has given me hope! It's given me purpose! It's given me a reason to get up this morning and write the chapter on DEFEAT! Life is a lot more about the journey than it is the destination. (That chapter is forthcoming!) What are we destined for? We are destined for greatness! not DE-FEAT! The FEAT before me may seem large, but the GOD above me is bigger and more powerful. He loves us and wants us to live a victorious life absent of DE-pression.

While I write this, I am listening to worship music and Joyce Meyer says we need God's help in everything we do. The greatest victory of all followed what most would consider a great DEFEAT! Christ's death and burial in the grave was overcome by him overcoming the grave – a supernatural FEAT!

I am about to share a life event which easily could have buried me. We all have some experiences that might seem surprising to others, even shocking. Well, this is one of those events. I am going to be very vulnerable here!

The Biblical reference used to compare this experience is that of Joseph, when his brothers sold him into slavery. From there things only got worse. While working for Potiphar's wife, Joseph was wrongfully accused by her of a sexual assault. Joseph found himself in prison, but not without hope. I have yet to find where Joseph ever complained about his situations. He trusted GOD and knew GOD had the bigger plan.

I can't say the same. I was involved in a relationship with a GOD-less man. I knew better but justified it by hoping he would become a Christian. I was unevenly YOKED and the bible teaches against this. I found him prospecting other women and using pornography while we were living together, and I asked him to move out. Instead of moving on, I looked back! Much like Lot, my efforts turned to a pillar of salt. By and through a domestic incident, I was wrongfully accused of a crime. These events have given me a life experience to overcome with God's guidance, and I determined to put my energies into this book to help others examine their own experience with depression.

One life event, even two-life events, do not make for a lifetime of defeat. Whatever the FEAT, it can be dealt with BOLDNESS and Courage. Above all be yourself and stay true to your calling. The depression will lift. The event I'm speaking of could have caused me to be in a deeper well of despair, and I was, for a while. What man intended for my harm, GOD intends for my GOOD. Without the test, there would be no TESTIMONY!

I hope using these life stories and illustrations helps others realize they too can be an overcomer, regardless of their circumstances.

Chapter Ten: DE-FECTIVE

Imperfect or faulty
Similar: faulty, flawed, imperfect, not working, malfunctioning, out of order, deficient, deformed

Take the DE-out of Defective, turn life around ....to become the effective person you were meant to be. We are all unique! WE have our own little quirks, idiosyncrasies, and peculiarities. That's what makes us who we are.... There is not another one like you! Our imperfections don't have to be defects. We are all "Fearfully and Wonderfully Made" ....but what do we do on those days we are feeling "faulty"? But what happens when we aren't feeling quite like we used to, if our mood is low, and the brain feels like it's malfunctioning? Correct the defective thinking....

Maybe you're having a hard time today, ...remembering when life was good. Maybe you're in pain, physically and psychologically, and don't know what to do about it. You might be feeling a little ....De-fec-tive..

We all are!........None of us is perfect, no not one.......

Let me reiterate: God says he made us "FEARFULLY and WONDER-FULLY.

Psalms 139 verses 13-14: For it was You who created my inward parts: you knit me together in my mother's womb. I will praise you because I have been fearfully and wonderfully made."

I asked myself, how can anyone get or be Depressed knowing they were Fearfully and Wonderfully Made! Hummmm? Then my spirit, nudged me and said....do you really believe what you're writing and reading?

Then Praise Him! That's what was missing here. PRAISE him! PRAISE HIM!

I was raised exposed to multiple denominations one being Southern Baptist...and we sang a little song that went like this......Praise him praise him all ye little children God is love, God is love... Praise him praise him all ye little children God is love, God is love...!

How could anyone feel defective and depressed if they take the morning to thank and praise God. For the air we breathe, for the skies we see, for the good things he has brought to our lives.

A Defect is an imperfection....we are perfect in his sight. FEARFULLY and WONDERFULLY so.

We are made by God's Design....he planned us to be knit in our mother's womb.

I taught Biology in High School for 16 years. One of my favorite units to teach was genetics. Our DNA is what makes us FEARFULLY and WONDERFULLY made.

The combinations of DNA are limitless to create a new human being... no one's DNA is the same.

Sometimes mutations occur which could result in imperfections. A perfect example is incomplete dominance...which results in a blending of both traits. My point is your mother and father both contributed to your physical traits and make you unique.... a RED and WHITE flower cross to make a PINK carnation.

What could be perceive as a DE-fect is actually a beautiful new color. We can take this analogy and translate this into taking one of our seemingly undesirable qualities or traits and working to make ourselves more effective.

Anything involving "self-improvement" takes time.... Fitness and weight loss complement each other to make one more "effective". Usually when someone makes a goal to lose weight it's with the goal of self-improvement! Remember the slightest change can be an improvement.

Try not to quantify your progress, but instead qualify it! Give yourself credit! When no one else is there to affirm you, affirm yourself. You are fearfully and wonderfully made!

Take the DE-out of Defective and become more Effective by recognizing your Uniqueness!

Chapter Eleven: DE-FINE

1. state or describe exactly the nature, scope, or meaning of.
Similar: explain, expound, interpret, describe, give the meaning of
2. mark out the boundary or limits of
Similar: determine, establish, fix, specify, designate, decide, stipulate

Take the DE- out of define and you'll be FINE.

Don't let someone else DEFINE who you are.

Don't let your past DEFINE you, let it prepare you for a better future.

Say this prayer: Do what you want to do in me, so you can do what you're going to do through me.

God has told us who we are! We are his children!

You don't have to "feel" confident to be confident! Your confidence rests in God, step out in faith

Who do people say that I am? Response: Some say that thou art John the Baptist, some, Elias, and others, Jeremiah, or one of the prophets, who do you say that I am? Simon, Peter answered and said, "Thou art the Christ, the Son of the living God."

Jesus answered and said unto him, "Blessed art thou, Simon....for flesh and blood hath not revealed it unto thee, but my Father which is in heaven." *(Matthew 16:13)*

Reflect on this passage for a moment and apply it to yourself. Who do people say you are? You might get a different answer depending on who you ask. If it is just easy for your perception of yourself to adjust, then maybe you need to quit asking others their opinion, because your identity will shift like the tides with every opinion you get. Sticks and stones may break my bones, but names last will always hurt me. It not just that they hurt, but other's opinions of you are usually limiting. Remember, they have a limited perspective, limited access, and limited mentality. God's opinion of us is we are "fearfully and wonderfully made" and if that isn't enough, we are made in his image!

Blessed are you, for flesh and blood have not revealed this to you, but my God in heaven. Peter was the only disciple who got out of the boat! Forget what lies behind and stop living in the shadow of your past!

Take the De out of De-fine and you'll be "fine!" Follow your purpose and following your passion! (Philippians 3:13-14.)Be not conformed, be transformed by the renewing of your mind (Philippians 2:2)

Be not unequally yoked

Psalms 139:14

Luke 15: 17 He came to himself........ Proper perspective...

Genesis 50:20

Zechariah: not by power by spirit.

Jeremiah 29

I listened way too long to what others thought of me, and some of you have, too! Listen to your heart! There's a message in every beat, the rhythm of who you are and who you were intended to be, minus all the opinions of others, equals God's view of who you are, fearfully and wonderfully made. Your uniqueness adds a new dimension to someone else's life, including your own. Be careful who you let tell you what they think of you! Jealousy, resentment, and spite drives many a good human being into judging others.

Determination– Determine to know him, and you will know yourself better!

Luke 15:17, Father I have sinned against God. He spent all he had.

Job 19:25, I know my redeemer and my vindicator lives!

Imagine, what it must have taken for Job to believe what he was saying when he had lost so much. The devil can throw his best shot at you, but know like Job knew!

Rehabilitate:

Be still and know that I am God … *(Psalms 46:10)*

Jolted awake in the middle of the night by racing thoughts, it's like the demons are hard at work to prevent me from getting the kind of sleep which restores the mind and the body. The consequence of these awakenings is, when I do finally wake up, I'm exhausted from wrestling with the demons in my thoughts. People who suffer from depression often have sleep disturbances. It's kind of a paradox Do the sleep disturbances cause the depression? Or does the depression cause the sleep disturbances? So, what is a person to do? I have a combination of suggestions, any one of these or the combination can be used to promote rehabilitative sleep.

Take a supplement that contains GABA, melatonin, valerian root, calcium and/or magnesium. Exercise to the state of near exhaustion in late afternoon, but not too late to be stimulating. Swimming or water exercise can be calming and reduce muscle tension or yoga for relaxation or flexibility. You really have to look for and find something that works for you.

Shut the T.V. off and read before bedtime. Though reading can be stimulating, select a book that doesn't stir your thoughts or is emotionally provoking. Learn to meditate and be in the moment. Find a favorite scripture and meditate on it.

Some suggestions are:

God has not given us a spirit of fear … but of power, and of love, and of a sound mind *(2 Timothy 1: 17)*.

Peace, I leave with you, my peace I give unto you. Let not your heart be troubled, neither let it be afraid. John 14:27

I appreciate the Bible apps which provide us with such instant scripture, though there's nothing quite like the "written word." In a pinch, this works. I use the KJV Bible app.

Take a very warm to hot bath, use lavender to create a spa effect. Lavender is the herb for calming. You might laugh at this suggestion, but I discovered a lavender baby lotion when I nannied my grandson, Ollie, several years ago. There are actually two, Johnson and Johnson makes one, and OGX Beauty from Walgreens. Now there are also essential oils available and some can be made into teas or taken sublingual (under the tongue.) I also have a pillow spray which I mist before climbing into bed. Any or all of these in combination can be used for a natural sleep remedy.

Take the De - out of Define: Don't let others, events, or situations define who you are, and you'll be ....FINE.

Chapter Twelve: DE-FINITION

a statement of the exact meaning of a word

1) Depression is a state of low mood and aversion to activity.
2) A mental health disorder characterized by persistently de-pressed mood or loss of interest in activities, causing significant impairment in daily life. (National Network for Depression Centers)

Similar Description:
Possible causes include a combination of biological, psychological, and social sources of distress. Increasingly, research suggests these factors may cause changes in brain function, including altered activity of certain neural circuits in the brain. (Neurophysiologist, Dr. Caroline Leach) I'm presenting an additional perspective on Depression which investigates and includes the spiritual component.

The persistent feeling of sadness or loss of interest which characterizes major depression can lead to a range of behavioral and physical symptoms. These may include changes in sleep, appetite, energy level, concentration, daily behavior, or self-esteem. Depression can also be associated with thoughts of suicide.

The American Psychological Association defines depression as, "a negative affective state, ranging from unhappiness and discontent to an extreme feeling of sadness, pessimism, and despondency, that interferes with daily life."

An Our World In Data study estimates about 3.4% (margin of error makes this range 2%-6%) of the global population has depression. This is about 264,000,000 people worldwide. Those are staggering statistics. According to WHO estimates, the ten countries with the highest prevalence of depression are:

Ukraine (6.3%)
United States (5.9%)
Estonia (5.9%)
Australia (5.9%)
Brazil (5.8%)
Greece (5.7%)
Portugal (5.7%)
Belarus (5.6%)
Finland (5.6%)
Lithuania (5.6%)

I could drown you with statistics on depression, but here are just a few provided by the National Network for Depression Centers founded in the United States.

1. We lose about as many people to suicide as we do to breast cancer, annually.

2. Two-thirds of people with depression do not seek nor receive proper treatment. (2015)

3. Lost earnings from mental illness is 210 Billion.... $210,000,000,000.00 a year. (2017)

4. Depression is the leading cause of disability in the United States between the age of 15-44 years old.

5. Depression ranks among the top 3 workplace issues in the United States along with Stress.

Take out the DE-finition......and don't let Depression have the final word.

Though what I have provided you is a very clinical perspective of depression, I intend to help you realize depression doesn't have to have the "final word."

Take the De- out of definition and the final word is "finition." Break that down, -tion is the suffix which means a process.

Finite means the final... or has an end. Your life does not have to begin or end with depression. Low mood and lack of activity can be improved by getting more "active." By taking a proactive stance in your own mental health treatment. Also, physical activity is proven to benefit any mental health disorder. I'll address this in a later chapter.

Take the first STEP: START, TODAY, EMBRACING, the PROBLEM. This is why we never give up.

"Our spirits are being renewed every day, and our present troubles are small and won't last long. Temporary problems are going to produce an everlasting reward. Fix our eyes on not what is seen, but what is unseen" (*11 Corinthians 4:16-18*).

Depression also has a Spiritual component. We will address that in another chapter I call, *De-vil*. Take the DE-out of Devil and unmask the evil behind the thoughts.

1) Spirit renewed. Meditate on the word.
2) Know that all troubles are temporary.
3) Know that God is using everything to build character for our "GOOD."
4) Great is the reward and is an eternal reward.
5) Focus on God and not on the problems, or focus on a higher-power, and not on the problem.

This book is going to contain an abundant number of affirmations and scripture which I recommend become a part of your daily routine. Each chapter can be read in sequence, or you can pick one and make it your daily focus! You can even develop your own DE-word for the day and find scripture which applies. I was amazed at the unfolding of this book, as it expanded from an original twelve chapters to what is currently in your hands!

I woke up this morning, with all kinds of voices in my head. You know the ones, from "it's too cold to get out of bed," to "you really don't know what you're saying," to "you're stuck in this chapter," and "you know editing and organizing are your biggest challenge," to "nobody is going to want to read what you have to say." I stopped and prayed, "God bring to me today what you would have me say." Then I went to my email for *Daily Hope* by Rick Warren. I needed to hear what he had to say today. Without fail, God has guided my efforts.

"Trust in the LORD with all your heart and lean not on your own understanding" (*Proverbs 3: 56.*)

"In all your ways acknowledge him, and he shall direct your paths."

As I shared this morning, the "voices" in my head were not of GOD. I had to trust in what GOD has in store for me (for us) and get up and write. I committed to writing two hours (or more) daily until this book was submitted for publishing. This morning I had to wage war on the De-vil and the negative thoughts in my mind. There are days you will likely have to do the same! When Jesus spoke to Lazarus he said, "GET UP!" John 11 tells the story. Lazarus was allowed to die, before Jesus took action, and raised him from the dead. We can be totally De-motivated, but when our faith is placed and we acknowledge him, he can "raise" us from this dead place.

We can't let the De-vil, or evil thoughts destroy our motivation, "get up and GO", because it is not GOD's desire. If we want to defeat depression, we need to take charge! Take action.

He will direct your path and give you the energy to accomplish his task.

Take the DE- out of Depression and PRESS ON!

Chapter Thirteen: DE-FORMED

Adj. (of a person or part of the body) not having the normal or natural shape or form; misshapen
Similar: contort, distort, and warp.

Can we take a deformed mind and reform it? Or better yet, transform it?

Yes, we can! It's going to require changing some DE-words into positive forms of these words to give new life or meaning to them! The LORD declares, "For I know the plans I have for you, plans to give you a hope and a future!" Depression tends to deform our thoughts and beliefs, so we lose our motivation, our beliefs become bygones, our desires become defective, our hearts become heavy, our minds are "messed up," and left to our own demise and our thoughts become DEFORMED. We all have seen this in a physical sense. You might have even had a close friend or relative that had a "birth deformity"; a disfigurement of a physical feature on the body, whether external or internal. One out of 33 babies (between 2% and 3%) born in the United States are affected by birth defects. The number increases to 5% by age one (www. cdc.gov).

These types of deformities can impact a person for life, unless they receive some form of corrective surgery or surgeries. Many times it takes multiple surgeries to correct the deformities as a person matures. Consider this: 1 out of

4 people use braces to correct some imperfection in their bites or smiles. Elective or necessary, this corrective process takes time, the assistance of professional expertise, and usually 6 months to 3 years (LA Dental). But look at the new smile which is transformed as a result of "bracing" the teeth. I've never had braces, but I have worn a cast to repair broken bones. The physician "sets" the bones into alignment, it forces the broken ends to stay in place long enough for the bones to mend and become strong again. So what if we were to give the same consideration to the "deformed" personality or psychological feature?

Once again, I must state a disclaimer. I'm not a psychologist or psychiatrist, but I have had experiences with a spectrum of them as I pursued my mental health healing. If you decide to embark in the process of mental health evaluation, I would suggest you get more than one opinion. Consistency in the diagnoses helped me settle into acceptance and treatment plan. Also, doctors and psychologists specialize in the treatment of different disorders. One way to curtail some of the medical expense is by listening to experts who participate in online education and podcasts while you might be determining a course of action. Don't delay too long, as some symptoms can become worse without treatment if they are truly rooted in an organic problem or brain chemistry.

Deformity of personality: Nature vs. Nurture

An infant comes into this world from the very self-contained, sheltered environment of the womb. But if exposed to drugs or a lack of nutrition, might have physical or neurological defects which can cause impediments in physical and psychological maturing and growth, but what about the development of personality or mental illness? Most theorists agree personality is primarily formed after birth. Some believe there is a genetic predisposition toward some mental illnesses. This definition of personality supports this theory.

Personality is the characteristic sets of behaviors, cognitions, and emotional patterns that evolve from biological and environmental factors.

If you seek professional help for depression, the clinician is likely to use a battery of tests or assessments to evaluate and determine what they deem is an appropriate diagnosis in an effort to chart a "plan of action," or treatment plan. Most treatment plans include some form of "talk therapy" with a mental health practitioner, albeit a psychiatrist, licensed psychologist, social worker, or therapist of your choosing.

Sometimes we are limited by health insurance, but many therapists practice what is called a sliding scale to meet the financial needs of their patients or clients. I encourage you to seek the assistance of a professional mental health practitioner to meet your specific needs.

What causes the malformation or deformed personality; life events, traumas, abuse, psychological, physical, drugs, or neglect (deprivation), or a combination of these.

While some depression may come from a physiological (organic) origin, like a chemical imbalance in the brain, in my experience treating depression needed to include evaluating family history, life events, traumas, relationships, physical illness or injury, and nutrition. It was when I started addressing the deep spiritual component and "deformed" thought processes I began to experience the truest personal break through.

Dr. Carolyn Leaf, Neurophysiologist, describes the process of "Cleaning up your Mental Mess" to reduce anxiety, depression, and toxic-thinking in your mind. Dr. Leaf's theory and philosophy from a basis of recognizing how powerful the mind is, and "re-wiring" our thought processes. The mind is a part of the spirit man, while the brain is the physical organ which requires a fine-tuned balance of neurotransmitters to perform at its peak.

Few modern day therapies address the "spiritual" component in the treatment of depression. Though I was raised in a Classic Judeo-Christian environment, and well-versed in Biblical teachings and scripture, I grew to value the life applications more as I began exploring and researching depression while in the middle of the 2019 Covid Pandemic.

The one thing that stood out to me was the commonality of how we form better, yet De-form our thoughts which impact our mental health and emotions, many of which are subconscious or subliminal in nature. My therapist, Glenda Bates, a licensed Mental Health Counselor, addressed the theory of

"Core Beliefs." These beliefs are a person's most central ideas about themselves, others, and the world. These beliefs are formed in our early formative years and lay the foundation to beliefs acquired throughout our lifetime.

These beliefs can be "deformed" based on the way we are raised, lack of physical and emotional nurturing, life experiences, and trauma. All of which can lay a foundation for depression. I use scriptures from the Amplified Bible to support: God has not given us a spirit of FEAR, but of power, and of love, and of a sound mind (*2 Timothy 2:7*).

I believe much of my depression is based in fear and trauma. The fear developed from events, traumas, criticisms of others, and double mindedness which accompanies fear. In order to better understand your personal experience, I believe taking a personal inventory is a good place to start. I write a chapter about DE-ep – digging deep. There will be some tough questions which you are going to have to face the answers to if you expect to make progress out of depression.

Stop and ask yourself, what am I afraid of? Some of us are afraid of failure while others are afraid of success. Some of us live in fear of our family members or spouses, people close to us who impute fear by criticism or control. Only you can ask and answer those deep questions about what you are fearful of and whether or not you're really ready to resolve them.

I was afraid to write this book. This fear came from deformed thoughts about my self-worth. Even while writing I've had to overcome the fear I wasn't worthy, educated enough, experienced enough … good enough. This is how I replaced those thoughts – scripture. GOD tells me, "I am fearfully and wonderfully made" (*Psalms 139*.) My thoughts can be "transformed" by the renewing of my mind! Ask yourself, where have your thoughts been deformed? and are you ready to reform them, or better yet, transformed them. I believe thoughts get deformed by three means of control: suppression, repression, and oppression, which leads to depression. If thoughts are deformed, then it makes sense there is a process which can reform them and transform our lives. Let's investigate the negative processes which can influence the formation of our thoughts and beliefs.

<u>Suppression</u>: the action of suppressing something such as an activity or publication.

Similar: conquering, vanquishing, repression, crushing, quelling, quashing, squashing, prevention, censorship, keeping secret, concealment. hiding, smothering, stifling, muzzling, banning, nondisclosure, restriction

Any way you look at suppression it is a form of preventing someone or something from developing normally. Suppression is caused by an outside force or influence. As I apply this to depression, anyone who has been suppressed from being themselves is more likely to experience depression. The opposite of Suppression is freedom and unlimited growth.

<u>Repression</u>:

1) the action of subduing someone or something by force.

Similar: domination, tyranny, subjection, dictatorship, authoritarianism, censorship

Opposite: freedom, liberty

2) the restraint, prevention, or inhibition of a feeling, quality, etc. "the repression of anger can be positively harmful"

Similar: restraint, holding back, keeping back, biting back, control, keeping under control, stifling, smothering, bottling up, inhibition, frustration

Opposite: expression

the action or process of suppressing a thought or desire in oneself so that it remains unconscious.

Look at repression seriously. If your freedoms, liberty, or personal expression were prohibited, you are probably more inclined to live in fear and be depressed.

Finally, let's take a look at oppression as a factor which leads to depression.

<u>Oppression</u>:

1) prolonged cruel or unjust treatment or control.

Similar: persecution, abuse, maltreatment, ill treatment, enslavement, exploitation, cruelty, harshness, brutality, injustice, hardship, misery, suffering, pain, anguish, wretchedness
Opposite: freedom, democracy

2) the state of being subject to unjust treatment or control.

Similar:
3) mental pressure or distress.

Suppression, repression, and/or oppression, any one or any combination of these, can lead to depression. Exposure to repression, suppression, and oppression can contribute to deforming our thought processes. What can we do to reform or transform them into positive, healthy thoughts which lead to changes in our mental health and alleviate depression. It's important to recognize if these methods of control were used in your life and potentially caused stunted emotional growth, deformed personality traits, and inhibited your own personal emotional maturation process. Claim back what was taken from you as a form of "reforming" your thoughts and transforming your life to leave depression behind you!

As suggested in Ephesians 6:11-18, "One way to do this is to take on the armor of GOD, to fight against the Satan and the evils of the world. Our struggle is not against flesh and blood, but against the rulers, against the authorities, against the powers of this dark world, and against the spiritual forces of evil in the heavenly realms." So, when the day of evil comes, you'll be able to "stand your ground." Stand firm then ... This armor includes the belt of truth (not the lies the world or the devil would have you believe), the breastplate of righteousness (do what is right and good and you will not have regrets), your feet fitted with readiness from the gospel of peace (willingness to serve), the shield of faith (trusting God for what you cannot see), the helmet of salvation (protection of your mind against false teachings), and the SWORD of the Spirit, which is the Word of God (so you're armed to replace the negative thoughts with God's truth). Imagine the battle we could wage on depression if we put this armor on every evening when we retire and morning when we awake.

I hope the Scriptures I have employed guide you into a place of hope, peace, and love, which will aid in your pursuit of healing from depression.

Take the DE- out of Deformed and reform our thoughts and ideals of ourselves. Transform our lives for the service of God and others.

Chapter Fourteen: DE-LAY

1) to Postpone, put off until another time
2) to keep from being on time
Similar: detain, hold up, make late, retard, keep (back), holdup,
wait

De-lay? We live in a society built on instant gratification – high speed internet, six lane freeways at 75 MPH, and instant microwaveable foods. Don't get me wrong, it can all be good, until we forget **a minor delay doesn't constitute a major problem**. Even the video conferencing commonly used is titled ZOOOOOOOM! I read a quote once, "You're lack of planning does not constitute my emergency." There are times when a delay is good, but there are times when a delay can be very costly. Let's gain some perspective on when taking the DE- out of Delay could be to our benefit or to our demise.

Delaying gratification usually brings about heightening of the gratification. If we put off tasting the cherry pie on Thanksgiving until our dinner is settled, the cherry can taste oh so much sweeter. Clearing our pallet of other tastes and aromas allows us to experience the full effect of the tart, sweetness of the cherries, though it requires a delay in the process.

I remember a time when I was caught up in a traffic jam and delayed to my destination, only to find the cause of the delay was a fifteen car pile-up. If

I had left sooner, without delay, I might have been caught up in the wreckage and injured. Delays can also cause anxiety to creep and create doubts. DE-lay. When a Delay is brought about, we can take a different perspective. Maybe it's God's way of protecting us. Postponement can prevent disasters from happening. Taking the DE- out of delay. "Cast [lay] all your cares on him because he cares for us." 1 Peter 5:7.

Psalms 55:22 says it another way, "Cast your cares on the LORD and he will sustain you; he will never let the righteous be shaken."

Delays have a way of unnerving us by taking things that were in our control out of our control. However, when we take the DE- out of delay, and rest in him instead of our circumstances, we can maintain calm. Waiting can make us weary, but Matthew puts it like this: "Come to me, all you who are weary and burdened, and I will give you rest." You can find rest in your circumstances knowing God gives it to us. Sometimes there's no predicting when good things or terrible things are going to happen. Delays are certain.

Ecclesiastes 3: 1-8, reminds us,

"To everything there is a season,

a time for every purpose under heaven;

a time to be born, and a time to die,

A Time to plant, and a time to pluck what is planted;

a time to kill, and a time to heal;

a time to break down, and a time to build up;

A time to weep and a time to laugh;

A time to mourn and a time to dance;

a time to cast away stones , and a time to gather stones;

a time to embrace, and a time to refrain from embracing;

a time to gain, and a time to lose;

a time to keep, and a time to throw away;

A time to tear, and a time to sew;

a time to keep silence, and a time to speak;

a time to love, and a time to hate; and

a time of war and a time of peace."

Delays could be just another opportunity to reevaluate and reflection the direction our lives are going, potentially bringing about change.

When can a delay contribute to our demise? Is there anyone out there who deals with procrastination? A type of delay. Let me apply this to the delay in medical treatment of any kind. The delay of treatment, going into denial, can result in an emergency. Chest pain, shortness of breath, tightness, numbness, and tingling in either arm can be preliminary indicators of a bigger problem if you delay. A heart attack!

During the pandemic, I stumbled across podcasts from some reputable clinical and counseling psychologist who specializes in depression, anxiety, and post-traumatic stress disorder (PTSD). I found these forms of "therapy" very helpful, both from an educational perspective and from a means of identifying symptoms which would encourage someone into a place of taking action and seeking treatment.

Procrastination is a means of delaying or postponement often out of fear of the unknown. When it comes to our health, procrastinating about treatment can actually cause a furtherance or progression of the disease, which makes it more difficult to treat! Please don't delay! If you have any of the symptoms of depression, anxiety, or PTSD, check out these podcasts to self-access and don't hesitate to take action. Delays in treatment and delays in diagnosis are delays toward healing!

MedCircle provides a list of providers:

Dr. Les Carter, PhD, Counseling psychologist

Dr. Ramani Durvasula, PhD, Clinical psychologist - another provider who I have recently enjoyed her approach to education.

Anna Runkle, *Crappy Childhood Fairy* and cPTSD.

Ultimately, there is no true replacement for having a tried and trusted relationship with a therapist of your choice.

Take the DE- out of Delay and Lay aside your fears, and cares. Seek counsel, seek treatment, seek a healing today!

Chapter Fifteen: DE-LIVERANCE

1. the action of being rescued or set free.
Similar: liberation, release, freeing, rescue, discharge, emancipation, salvation, redemption

The Lord's Prayer says it best, "Deliver us from Evil," for thine is the kingdom, power, and glory forever.

Isaiah 42:16, "I will lead the blind by the way they do not know. I will guide them in paths that they do not know. *I will make darkness into light before them*. And rugged places into plains. These things I will do (for you) and I will not leave them abandoned or undone." What an incredible promise GOD makes to his people through Isaiah. When I need lifting up, I remember another scripture in *Isaiah, 40:31*, "Those that wait on the Lord...renew your strength."

Ask yourself, where is your darkness? What is confusing to you? Where is your spirit suppressed, repressed, and/or oppressed?

A part of the deliverance process is figuring out what you need deliverance from.

Many 12-step programs recommend taking a personal inventory. Ask yourself some tough questions and dig deep into the alcoves of the hurts, habits, and hang-ups which may be holding you down.

Healing from Depression involves a process of identifying those things you want to be delivered from. This book is intended to be a guide based on my own experiences and revelations, insights, and applications of all of the options available to help heal the "whole" person – mind, body, and spirit.

Many people are tormented by their secrets. Keeping secrets stored inside is a form of suppression. Humans by and through a series of events, there is a lot of evil in the world. Guilt, shame, and regret are emotions which rob us of JOY. They are "dark" emotions. Guilt is the feeling you did something bad. Shame is "YOU are bad." Either way, when these emotions are dealt with to alleviate our emotions of the burden of carrying them. Ridding ourselves of feelings of guilt, shame, and regret is a move in the right direction. GOD wants to deliver us from those emotions. They are strongholds which can lead to depression. I believe we can be "rescued," delivered from these negative emotions.

Rick Warren teaches a podcast lesson on coming out of the darkness and into the light, *"The Light of Jesus at Christmas Time."* I highly recommend this podcast found in *Pastor Rick's Daily Hope.*

He says, "Light is life to anything living." The sun is our source of physical light, God's son is our source of spiritual light.

Many people today feel trapped by their addictions, their secret compulsions. There is a way to be delivered from these burdensome mindsets and emotions. But there is also a God of hope and deliverance.

My first visit to see, my initial psychiatric physician, I was referred by my former employer for a second opinion. Dr. Lucas Van Orden asked me why I was there. Through the course of discussion, I revealed I was optimistic I could be **healed** of my depression. He commented it was highly unusual to have a patient express a desire for healing, as it was more common for them to be dependent on medications. The healing is there for the asking. The Deliverance I believe David spoke of was not just deliverance from physical harm. It was quite apparent David was in touch with his emotional side and spiritual side and he went to God with all of his request, as he was known as the man after God's own heart. In *Psalms 23: 4*, Even though I walk through the "dark" valley of the shadow of death.

I will fear no evil, for you are with me, your rod and staff comfort and console me." The great Shepherd David speaks of "delivers" his sheep (us) from darkness, dangers, and evils of this world.

The same GOD can shepherd us, can deliver us, from the evils of any secret, addiction, emotion, thoughts, or feelings which result in depression. Deliverance is available for those who believe … This thought aligns with the scripture.

John 8:12" I am the light of the world. If you follow me, you won't have to walk in *darkness*, because you will have the light that leads to life."

Reflecting on what Jesus said to the crowds who follow him, surely if we adopted these spiritual truths depression cannot take a stronghold in our lives.

Let's take a quick look at the Beatitudes of Christ, *Matthew 5*. I am citing from the Amplified Bible.

"Blessed (spiritually prosper, happy) are the poor in spirit (humble), for theirs is the kingdom of heaven.

Blessed (refreshed by God's grace) are they that mourn, for they shall be comforted.

Blessed (inwardly peaceful) are the meek (kind-hearted), for they shall inherit the earth.

Blessed (joyful) are they which do hunger and thirst after righteousness, for they shall be filled.

Blessed (content) are the merciful, for they shall obtain mercy.

Blessed (mature) are the pure in heart, for they shall see GOD.

Blessed (spiritually calm with life joy) are the peacemakers, for they shall be called the sons of GOD.

Blessed (morally courageous) are the they which are persecuted for righteousness sake, for theirs is the kingdom of heaven."

These are Christ-like qualities which, if sustained, are followed by promises. Then he says, "We are the salt of the earth, but if salt loses its flavor it is not good for anything." This is why deliverance from depression is so essential! Because if we lose our effectiveness, or motivation, or JOY, or purpose, and ultimately some lose their lives, we aren't good for anything. The devil wins! Evil wins! We can't let that happen, and we don't have to.

Ask GOD for a deliverance, be set free, then take the de- out, take on the beatitudes and learn to live again! Be blessed instead of the "mess" depression would have us believe we are.

"God can make greatness out of a great mess," Joel Osteen March 2, 2014. He related the story of Ishmael, the son of Abraham by his slave Hagar. Boy, was Sarah mad, hence the ultimatum. In the end, God brought a great nation out of Ishmael.

They may have put you at a disadvantage, .but you don't have to stay there. What could take a lifetime can happen in a split second with the favor of God. It's yours for the asking. Be Delivered.

Chapter Sixteen: DE-MEAN, DE-VALUE, DE-MORALIZE

(I'm combining these words because they have a common thread.....the spoken word.

The power of the spoken word to be destructive or constructive is remarkable.)

* Demean: cause a severe loss in the dignity of and respect for (someone or something).
Similar: degrading, shaming, humiliating,
* do something that is beneath one's dignity.

* Devalue: reduce or underestimate the worth or importance of.
Similar: belittle, depreciate, disparage, denigrate, bad-mouth

* Demoralize:
* 1. cause (someone) to lose confidence or hope; dispirit.
Similar: dishearten, dispirit, deject, cast down, depress

Many of us grew up hearing things which were not true about us. Have you ever been called a liar when you knew you had not lied? Have you ever been accused of something, just because someone else didn't like you or they were jealous of you. Being falsely accused, or labeled or name-called can impute personal doubt. Doubt once built upon can lead to questioning one's own identity. The furtherance of the loss of identity can lead to depression.

How many of us grew up saying or hearing this phrase, *"Sticks and stones may break my bones, but names will never hurt me."*

Many of us grew up with the saying that resonated in our ears when someone called us a name. It's not a matter of *if* you get called a name, it is a matter of *when* someone calls you a name.

One of the tragedies of this generation of school children has public awareness as "bullying," which often involves name-calling. Kids can be some of the cruelest, whether intentionally or unintentionally. When the damage is done, it's hard to overcome. But it's not impossible. As a matter of fact, Paul spoke to this, "ALL things are possible, through Christ who strengthens." ***Philippines 4:13***

Name-calling is defined as "abusive language or insults." In a lot of cases, children don't know how deeply the impact has been until later in life. We hear it in every aspect of society, all the way up to political candidates calling each other names during campaign events. It doesn't matter how remedial it may seem. It hurts! If you grew up hearing someone call you a "brat," or labeled you, there is a high likelihood you haven't shed the negative impact it has had on your self-esteem.

Scenario:

I taught school for sixteen years and had to address the needs of many students. One very common concern which has developed over the years is the impact of "attention deficit disorder" on learning ability. I had a young man tell me one day he couldn't learn math because he had ADD. My comment was it was up to him to order his thoughts and if he "bought into" that disordered thinking it would perpetuate the problem. I've reflected on what I said many times since. I believe when we unnecessarily label something, especially in children who take on the label as if it were their identity.

When someone uses name calling or labeling it can demonstrate a lack of appreciation, loss of dignity and loss of respect for one's self, develop a sense of unworthiness and unfulfilled dreams because of what others have said or done to you. When someone is demeaned, devalued, or demoralized, regardless of which it is, the foundation can be laid for depression.

I want to tell you today, you are enough! You are not what someone else thought or called you. You do have meaning! You do have value! You have a spirit, have a morale (either positive or negative belief about yourself.) We were designed in God's image, in Genesis, in the beginning. Genesis 1:26-27,"*God created man in His own image, in the image and likeness of GOD. He created him; male and female created them.*" God created Man and woman with a spirit-being. When we see, hear, and act upon things that demean, devalue, and demoralize us, we are reduced to something or someone GOD has not intended us to be. There are those who have not "self-actualized," they haven't realized their potential. They have believed what other people said they were.

Let's take the DE- out of Devalue, Demeaning, and Demoralizing, and use the following scriptures to give meaning, value, and morale.

Chapter Seventeen: DE-MOLISH

1. pull or knock down (a building.)
2. comprehensively refute (an argument or its proponent.)
3. overwhelmingly defeat (a player or team.)
Similar: destroy, obliterate, annihilate put an end to, smash, crush, squash, refute, do for

Corinthians 10:4-5 - Amplified Bible
The weapons of our warfare are not physical (weapons of flesh and blood.) Our weapons are divinely powerful for the destruction of fortresses. We are destroying sophisticated arguments and every exalted and proud thing that sets itself up against the true knowledge of GOD, and we are taking *every thought and purpose captive* to the obedience of Christ."

Throughout my efforts to write this book, I will go to a reference, whether a scripture or a definition for a DE-word, and I'll be exposed to another DE-word! So when I came across the scripture in 2 Corinthians 10 which used the word, "Demolish," I stopped, reflected, and finally looked up the definition. The King James version of the Bible uses the words, "Casting down imaginations."

Depression has a way of making you "feel" as if your out of control and it has taken over. That is the exact "imagination" this scripture is speaking of. Your feelings of depression are a form of deception. Whether the depression has an organic basis, from deregulated brain chemistry, or has been brought on by loss or some other unexpected life events, traumas, or other psychological impairments, ultimately the "feelings" which accompany depression can be impacted by making declarations, which are also known as affirmations.

Depression messes with the image GOD intended for us to have, the very image of him. We were created in his image! Neuroscientist Dr. Caroline Leaf says, "You have something you can do that no one else can do." She speaks of embracing your identity and getting down to your core basics. I highly recommend her podcast, episode 288: A Neurocycle, to improve low self-esteem and lack of confidence.

She refers to the brain as "Neuroplastic," having the ability to repair and grow the brain. In episode 320 she speaks of the changes in the brain when HOPE is used to build resilience. It is my hope we can create an approach to healing which addresses all the variables which potentially contribute to a person's ability to fight depression – mind, body (including the brain), and spirit.

One definition for demolish is a "comprehensively refute," another is a, "overwhelmingly defeat."

We can refute the negative thoughts that create fortresses (barriers) which prevent us from living productive, awe-inspiring lives – living with JOY! One way to do this is to implement change by making positive DE-clarations!

Affirmations:
"The LORD is a refuge and Stronghold for the Oppressed and a refuge in time of trouble!" (*Psalms 9:9*)r

And those who know Your name will put their confident trust in You. For You, O Lord, Have not abandoned those who seek You! (*Verse 9:10*)

He has not created us with a spirit of fear, but of sound mind! (*Timothy 1:7*)

Pulling down *strongholds* (bitterness, unforgiveness, obsessive worry, fear, jealousy, addiction, lust, adultery, meaningless intimate encounters, perfectionism, selfishness, fragile ego, despair or a complaining attitude, or such low confidence it prevents you from living the life GOD intended.)

A stronghold of the mind is *a lie Satan has established in our thinking we count as true but is actually a false belief.* When we embrace these lies, they affect our attitudes, emotions, and behaviors. Rebecca Greenwood has written a book, *Defeating Strongholds of the Mind*, which I'm recommending to gain more insight on the subject. The Bible describes a stronghold as a defensive structure; a refuge for the oppressed. So I'm a bit conflicted here. I've prayed for clarification. When someone is dealing with depression, I believe it has an origin in one of three areas: being oppressed, being repressed, or being suppressed leads to being depressed. When a person is hindered in their ability to be themselves, honor their true gifting (s) and talents, the own "place in this world," can lead to "feelings of loss and loneliness." Breaking down those Strongholds, is about "demolishing" those things, thoughts, and feelings, which keep us from experiencing personal growth and satisfaction.

If you're asking yourself, "Why does she quote the Bible so often?" The answer is there is no other book which provides a more comprehensive guide for living, and positive declarations given to us by and through the interpretations of men anointed by God to be the messengers.

This morning I read this quote by Eleanor Roosevelt, "With the new day comes new strength and new thoughts."

These Bible verses align with the aforementioned, "O LORD, O LORD, you have brought up my Soul from Sheol; *you restored me to life* from among those who *go down to the pit.* Sing praises to the LORD, O you his saints, and give thanks to his holy name. For his anger is but for a moment, and his *favor is for a lifetime.* Weeping may tarry for the night, but *JOY comes with the morning*! *(Psalms 30: 1-5)* (ESV)

And the JOY of the Lord is your Strength. (*Nehemiah 8:10*)

When we Demolish the old thoughts which accompany a depressed mind, we can experience a "renewing of our mind and new day every. Our day can begin with JOY in the morning!

"These things I have spoken to you that my JOY may be in you, and that your JOY may be made full." (*John 15: 10-11.)*

We have no true or lasting joy of our own. Therefore, when we rely on our own strength to take on the battle against depression, we are weak. But we can enter into the LORD's JOY and, therefore, be strong, and courageous in our efforts to overcome the enemy.

We can take the DE- out of demolish, leaving "molish". The English definition for molish is, "to please, pray, or ask. Let's take the DE- out of Demolish and use it to our benefit. Pray with expectancy and ask GOD to heal you!

Chapter Eighteen: DE-NIAL

1) The action of Declaring something to be untrue.

2) a statement that something is not true.

3) the refusal of something requested or desired.

Similar: refusal, withholding, withdrawal, rejection, dismissal

A psychological defense mechanism, postulated by Sigmund Freud, in which a person is faced with a fact too uncomfortable to accept, and rejects it instead, insisting it is not true, despite what may be overwhelming evidence.

You can't just wish it away, act like it's not there, or can you? Many of us have employed this defense mechanism at some time in our lives. Not sure what it will accomplish in the final outcome, but it certainly will work to avoid the issues for a while.

Scenario: Denial

I had a situation with a friend recently, where I suspected she attempted to "steal" my sunglasses. When I first noticed them missing, I had gotten back in my car after several brief stops while running errands. I commented to her about misplacing them and proceeded to turn my car upside-down in search of them. I looked in the console several times without locating them. Finally, I suggested I had left them back at the place I had visited first on our errand list. I went in while my friend waited in the car. No one in the bank had found them. I returned to the car and began looking again from the rear seat and floorboard when out of the blue, my friend held the sunglasses and another pair of reading glasses out toward me while asking, "are these them?" At first glance, I said no. Then, on further inspection, I recognized the sunglasses and happily retrieved them from her grasp.

Then the questions came. Where did you find them? "Under the socks in the console."

I accepted this at first, then it just didn't seem possible. I was in denial. Surely she wouldn't have taken them. But it all added up; there were several stops, she remained in the car while I ran inside, and then voile, the glasses appear. I couldn't deny the feelings which developed, and suspicion which remains.

I discussed the events with another person, who confirmed my suspicions. Have you ever heard the phrase, "If it walks like a duck, talks like a duck, smells like a duck, it is a DUCK!"

Consequently, the sunglass incident has left a sick feeling in my heart. Though I've forgiven her, and want to move on, the harsh reality was there.

There are more serious events which take place in a person's life that warrant our immediate attention, but many times we move into a denial phase to avoid the pain. Some of these include situations which may occur to us as children – sexual assaults, physical and emotional abuse, alienation, rejection, bullying. They can all have long term ramifications if we put off dealing with them, and instead choose to move into the defense mechanism of denial.

This was the case with myself. Healing can only occur when the matter is dealt with and forgiveness is rendered, if another person is involved. I've hesitated to tell the story, but feel it appropriate now.

Many celebrities have told their own personal stories of childhood abuse or sexual assaults only to have their audiences applaud their candidness and/or courage for being open and vulnerable. This is not always the reception one is met with when they decide to disclose such a personal event. Sometimes it just opens the victim up to many questions which instill guilt, blame, shame, and fault on the victim, as often happens when rape victims come forward. So, they (we) bury it by denying it rather than dealing with it. This can cause a manifestation of all kinds of other behaviors as a by-product of the event, such as eating disorders, self-loathing, self-destructive acts (e.g. cutting.) When we internalize these, emotions can develop into depression.

Scenario:

My story begins with the introduction of an older boy, then a senior in college, during my freshman year at college. He had paid particular attention to me when I would swim laps at the competition pool, as he was a lifeguard and member of the swim team. He suggested we go dancing sometime in a nearby city. The thought of a senior in college being attracted to me, was undeniably flattering, but I hesitated for a long time to accept. Then I did, and so we left for Little Rock one evening for a date of dancing and evening fun

He picked me up at my dorm and presented the opportunity to have a "rum and Coke." I was a novice at this drinking game, but thought it sounded harmless and I have to admit, it tasted quite good.

As the evening progressed, we found a neat little club alive with energy of great music and plenty to drink. I don't recall how many beverages I had, but I do recall mixing quite a few in a rather short period of time. That combined with the lack of experience I had was a formula for disaster.

I recall having a very difficult time getting back to the car, and then nodding off shortly after we got on the interstate headed back to my dorm. I recall pulling into the parking lot, having him go to the door to check if it was unlocked, having him come tell me I couldn't get in, driving to his apartment, being escorted upstairs, and waking up the next morning knowing I had been violated.

I called my former boyfriend and begged him to come get me. He did. I kept this incident suppressed inside for 10 years. I held it in denial. I blamed myself and lived with the guilt of it. Bottling it, stuffing it, denying it – will not fix it.

I have since received counseling, EMDR, and reconciled this event by offering forgiveness to the perpetrator, but the emotional scars are life-lasting. There's no way to know how many others were impacted by his behavior. However, I want to encourage anyone who has ever had a similar experience to seek counseling as soon as you read this, if you haven't already. I believe, in part, the foundation to depression or other mental illnesses can be rooted in these types of events, especially if not recognized for what they are. Those of us who deal with sexual assault can become the victor instead of the victim!

Look at the story of Jonah. I believe he was living in denial about what God had planned for him. Ultimately, he went to Ninevah and delivered the message, but not before he ran from the responsibility and landed in a Big Fish's belly. Yuck! If you are finding yourself in a place of denial, re-evaluate the costs of staying there. The sooner you deal, the sooner the heal!

How do you deal with someone who is in denial?

Talking with someone you love who's in denial may prove to be a challenge, but there are some ways to make it easier for both of you.

- Learn as much as you can
- See it differently
- Be gentle
- Practice nonjudgment
- Be an active listener
- Use 'I' statements
- Stay calm.

Let's Take the DE- out of Denial and move toward admission, radical acceptance, and move forward toward healing.

Chapter Nineteen: DE-NOUNCE

publicly declare to be wrong or evil.
"the Assembly denounced the use of violence"
Similar: condemn, criticize, attack, censure, discredit, damn, reject

By now you've caught on most of the words I use in this book are converted from a negative to a positive by taking the DE- out and turning the word around. Depression can also be treated in like fashion. We can turned it around with an aggressive approach to treatment, to attacking the evilness of its nature, and De-nouncing it.

I start my day by telling the depression it can't win! I tell it that it is of the devil and I've declared war on it. I can't tell you how many people I have encountered say they couldn't tell I have suffered with clinical depression. "You just don't seem the type", is what they say.

Well, depression doesn't know a type, socio-economic class, color, creed, or gender. It doesn't know whether you are right or left-handed. It simply does not discriminate. Pick one, any one of the words which are similar to De-nounce and use it to your advantage. Announce you are going to be victorious in your battles and the war on depression. Just as you can denounce the evil in depression, you can announce the victory.

The weapons of our war on depression require we not relinquish control of our minds. You have a God ordained right to enjoy your life, and the Devil doesn't want that to happen. When we are happy or joyful, the Devil is defeated. When we can be motivated to do what God wants us to do, the devil is defeated. Resist the Devil at his onset. Denounce his ability to steal our JOY. Announce, The JOY of the Lord is our strength!

The Devil moves slowly to impute doubt in our minds, which can develop into stronghold. We have the ability to halt the progression of disease by catching it before it becomes a stronghold. The Bible is one of the most positive sources we have to accomplish this. The more we equip ourselves with scripture, the more we are prepared to de-nounce the devil! Don't let depression take a stronghold in your life! Depression would have us believe we don't have a choice but to "feel" bad, sad, and defeated. Let's reverse this from happening.

Denounce. I found these scriptures under "Denouncing the Faith."
Revelation 12:9 ESV. And the great dragon was thrown down, that ancient serpent, who is called the devil and Satan, the deceiver of the whole world—he was thrown down to the earth, and his angels were thrown down with him.

1 Peter 5:8 ESV /Be sober-minded; be watchful. Your adversary the devil prowls around like a roaring lion, seeking someone to devour.

Announce: *Galatians 5:22-23 ESV* /But the fruit of the Spirit is love, joy, peace, patience, kindness, goodness, faithfulness, gentleness, self-control; against such things there is no law. *Romans 12:2* Do not be conformed to this world but be transformed (progressively changed) ....by the renewal of your mind. You are being transformed, changed so you might prove for yourself, what is the acceptable and perfect plan for you.

2 Corinthians 5:17 ESV /Therefore, if anyone is in Christ, he is a new creation. The old has passed away; behold, the new has come.

Especially, the last one. Denounce the one who would come to steal (your joy), kill (your ambition), and destroy (your life). Whether you determine to use scripture or other affirmations, announcing you are moving into a place of victory will lightened your mood, your day, your week. Get the mindset that depression will not defeat you. Find positive scripture, affirmations, and songs which will reflect you are announcing a victory! My therapist shared she listened to Donna Summers, "I'm Coming Out!" during a rough time in her life. I laugh, but this is the attitude I'm speaking of. To announce coming out of the darkness in a positive affirming way, even if the song is from a Billboard chart.

De-nounce the Devil and Defeat and **Announce** the Healing and Victory which comes when we claim it!

Chapter Twenty: DE-ODORIZE!

verb: remove or conceal an unpleasant smell
Similar: freshen, sweeten, purify, disinfect, sanitize, sterilize, fumigate

Have you ever driven past a landfill with your windows down? Initially, you might have wondered "where is that smell coming from?". Have you ever left the garbage unattended when you left town for a long trip, come home and opened the front door to "pew-wee!"...... Someone forgot to take the garbage out! Well, this is my story. While on a trip for the Holidays, I recruited some neighbors to watch my cats, Hans and Darth Vader. As a grave oversight, I left Gainesville, leaving Hans locked in the house. The neighbor called to inform me, he saw Hans sitting, meowing at the back door wanting out! The neighbor then went in to find the "*treasure* left on my bed. I was to be out of town through Christmas, 5 more days. Can you imagine the stench (let alone the angry kitty-cat), I would have returned to, if the neighbor had not discovered Hans. I will probably have to "de-odorize" my bed and bedroom (maybe the whole house) when I return.

So, let's take the example of the "landfill" that might have accumulated in a person's life. Whether it's happened because of our own decision-making or because others have dumped their trash or baggage in our lives, we all need to deal with the stuff. If we don't, the end result is an accumulation that could result in a "landfill" in our lives that produces a "stench", figuratively speaking something very unpleasant. Harboring resentment, bitterness, and grudges, and a spirit of unforgiveness (whether of ourselves or others), keeps our landfill, full of smelly thoughts and actions.

Get the stench out of your life!
I searched the Amplified Bible for "stench" and this is what I discovered,

"For those who are being lost, it is a deadly stench that kills; but for those who are being saved, it is a fragrance that brings life, and who is adequate and sufficiently qualified for these things." 2 Corinthians 2:16

How do we rid ourselves of the Landfill that's created such a stench in our lives. How do we de-odorized? Clean out the stuff creating the stench. Clean House. In the case, with depression, you might need to find the source of the stench. You might need to call on someone, or something else to clean house, empty your landfill. Let's start with the scripture aforementioned.... and the DE-sire. Pray that the spirit that has De-livered those that come before you is available for you. Call on another spirit to eliminate the spirit of Depression, the Holy Spirit. Let the Holy Spirit create the desire and "sire" you into this process.

Verse 14, says, " but thanks be to God, who always leads us in triumph.....and makes evident, the *sweet fragrance of the knowledge of him.*

I'm suggesting the following:
Read 2 Corinthians 2, in full so that you get the context of these suggestions.

1) Start with Confession...... Verse 2: " For if I cause you grief, who then provides me enjoyment but the very one whom I have made sad?" Whether you confess a sin, or confess a wrong against another person, the act of confession is very freeing. The act of confession "unloads" the burden of guilt or shame and/or hurting another human being. Confession of our sins is also considered an act of repentance toward being saved. When we don't confess, our "landfill" can accumulate stuff and the stench gets worse.

2) Lend Forgiveness. Verse 7, so instead (of further rebuke, now you should rather (graciously) **forgive** and comfort and encourage him, to keep him from being overwhelmed by excessive sorrow. Symptoms of Depression include a low mood, which I compare to "excessive sorrow". When we minister to others out of our own experiences, we alleviate ourselves of the "sorrow" that can weigh us down. Forgive….and let go. Verse 10: "If you forgive anyone anything, I too forgive (that one); and what I have forgiven if I have forgiven anything has been for your sake… This is a double whammy! You forgive and are forgiven! Forgiveness removes a heavy burden off of you physically, emotionally, and spiritually! It reduces the landfill…. the garbage. Forgiveness lifts the spirit of oppression. Confession and Forgiveness are forms of getting rid of the "stench", now let's consider replacing it with a new fragrance that is pleasing and positive to our mental health.

3) Give Comfort……. Verse 15: "For we are the sweet fragrance of Christ (which ascends) to God, discernible both among those who are being saved and among those who are perishing. When we comfort others, we are basically comforting ourselves, as it usually comes from a place of experiencing comfort, it's a chain reaction. Think of it as spiritual aromatherapy. Use of aromas can invoke a certain emotion. Lavender is calming (comforting). Lemon grass is up-lifting (encouraging). The scent of comfort, helps alleviate "sorrow". Someone who is experiencing Depression can feel isolated. Everyone benefits from being "comforted" that they are not alone in this life.

4) Encourage……Verse 7: "To keep him from being overwhelmed by sorrow." A natural by-product of encouraging others, is we are encouraged. It's almost like giving a compliment, that makes someone glow. It shines back in our direction, reflecting our positive comment. It is simple, so try not to over-think this. Compliments are a form of encouragement. 1 Thessalonians 5:11, "Encourage one another and build "one another" up just as you are doing. It is

reciprocal. Encouraged is used over 100 times in the New Testament. By comforting and encouraging others, we are less "self-focused" and more service focused. I speak to this in my chapter on De-serve.

The "stench of death" spoken of earlier, is liken to the feelings of not being worthy of living which can accompany Depression. We can get rid of and re-place those thoughts with thoughts brought about by confessing, forgiving, and replace them with acts of comforting, and encouraging others. These acts can build self-esteem. Your value, "your fragrance" which is sweet to those who, receive what you offer will replace the "stench" that developed from holding onto the garbage or burdens that had a stronghold on our minds.

In closing this chapter, De-Odorize by sharing your sweet fragrance of support and encouragement.

Chapter Twenty-One: DE-PRIVATION

the damaging lack of material benefits considered to be basic necessities in a society
2. the lack or denial of something considered to be a necessity.
Similar: poverty, impoverishment, penury, privation, hardship, destitution, need, indigence reduced circumstances.

When we think of the "necessities" of life what comes to mind? Those things that contribute to our Physical, Social, Psychological and Spiritual health and well-being. But what one person might consider a basic need, might be a luxury to another. For instance most of us, enjoy a hot bath or shower every day....but to many people it is not necessary to bathe every day. On the other hand, healthy nutrition, can impact every area of your life. Necessities are those things that are required or indispensable.

<u>Physical</u> things like, Food, and water, clothing and shelter. Those things that provide safety and security to a person's health and well-being.

<u>Social</u> connections? Friend and Family. Those connections that develop healthy social interactions.

Psychological elements? Nurturing, love, those things that develop a healthy mind.

Spiritual health and well-being. We are creatures of mind, body and spirit, so when we are deprived in one of the categories, it impacts all other areas of our life.

Deprivation can come from the lack of any source....or lack of something.

Philippians 4:19 And my God will supply all your needs according to his riches in glory.

If we believe that the same God still exists, the originator of life on this planet as we know it, then we must trust in him for our needs. Every one of them. Each breath, drink of water, and bite of food is supplied by his riches. We live in an abundant world. We truly have access to anything we want, let alone need. We just have to asked for it. God does not hold a magic wand, if you believe he is the creator, the healer, the master, our friend, we can ask him for our healing to and he will not deprive us of what we ask for.... but it may come over time. God is a GOD of miracles, but GOD also requires our participation in our healing. The great philosopher Oprah Winfrey, once said, "You get in life what you have the courage to ask for." While that may be true, and even biblical in some sense, as David said in Psalms 37, Verse 4 "Delight yourself in the Lord, and he will give you the desires and petitions of your heart. ⁵He will make your righteousness shine like the dawn, ⁶the justice of your cause like the shining of the noonday sun... ⁷Be still before the Lord, wait patiently for Him and entrust yourself to Him. .....⁸Cease from Anger and abandon wrath. Do not fret; it leads only to evil Finally, For those who do evil, will be cut off, but those who wait for the Lord, they will inherit the land. Also, in Isaiah 57:13, He who takes refuge in me will possess the land".

In Verse 15, " I dwell in the high and holy place, but also with the *contrite and humble in spirit*, in order to *revive the spirit of the humble* and to *revive the heart of the contrite*." With one exception, our emotional and psychological needs are often left up to our primary care givers in the developmental years. Human beings are very sensitive creatures that are dependent for "care-giving" longer than any other mammal. And probably the hardest to grasp....."For God so loved the world".........if you were raised in a church, you were exposed to this scripture very early on......John 3:16 I'm not a psychologist or sociologist, so I won't pretend to know the devastating impact of a lack of love and nurturing can cause in the developmental years, the evidence is in the prevalence of personality disorders and mental health disorders that plague our society.

Karen's story....
This is her own account to me in a phone conversation

There was no Christmas dinner that year..........She just couldn't get out of bed.....

She didn't know what brought it on....she couldn't quit crying.

I had done everything to make it a Christmas wonderland......3 hours of decorating...

I had invited people over for a prime rib dinner........

But, she got up Christmas morning unable to move.......

She summoned the energy to get up and watched the kids unwrap gifts......

It happened again when her son went into rehab.........her heart was broken......she was having to demonstrate "tough love"..... she had to.......and it was three days after his birthday and Christmas.

Two years in a row, Karen went through the same emotional and psychological mindset, without treatment.......

She said through the tear, "He thinks he's infallible"........"He's an addict".............What did I do wrong?

Karen was used to looking through rose-colored glasses.......Her main priority was to have a family, the white picket fence........the proverbial American dream.......

Her dream had turned into a nightmare due to drug addiction. It's preempted her depression.......she was in despair. Hopeless. Helpless. And desperately unhappy. She wanted to blame herself for her son's drug addiction, as many parents do. What could she have deprived her son of that caused him to turn to drugs? Maybe nothing.

Psalm 27:10 Though my father and my mother have forsaken me, my God will never forsake me."

"Your word is a lamp unto my feet, and a light unto my path". Psalms 119:105

When a person is depressed, they lose perspective of where the light comes from......There are days when all they can see is darkness and despair.

Also, in Psalms 57: 16, David recognizes, For I will not contend forever, nor will I always be angry, for (if I did stay angry) the spirit of man would grow weak before Me.......I have seen his willful ways, but I will heal him."

God doesn't not want us to live with a deprived spirit. When our spirit is deprived, all of our being is deprived. When cannot be deprived when we rest in his love. We were created for his love. For GOD so loved the world...

Take the DE-out of Deprivation, it leaves us privation.....a state in which things are essential for human well-being such as food and warmth.... hardship. There are times when we will go through hardship. But GOD does not intend for us to stay in the state of privation.

Instructions for how to lift depression are in assisting someone who is suffering from deprivation.

Psalms 59:3 Deliver me from my enemies........Depression is an enemy of your mental, physical and spiritual health and well-being.

Instructions for beating De-pression, are to served others.....but not to neglect ourselves in the process.

Isaiah 58:7 "Divide your bread with the hungry, bring the homeless poor into the house, when you see the naked, that you cover him, and not to hide yourself from the needs of your own flesh and blood!"

Listen to the promise that follows in Verse 8 if you follow Verse 7....."Then your light will break out like the dawn, and your healing (restoration, new life) will quickly spring forth, your righteousness will go before you (leading you to peace and prosperity), The glory of the LORD will be your rear guard."

Verse 10....again, "And if you offer yourself to (assist) the hungry, and satisfy the need of the afflicted, Then your light will rise in darkness, and your gloom will become like midday, and the LORD, will continually guide you, and *satisfy your soul in scorched and dry places* and *give strength to your bones*, and you will be like a watered garden, and like a spring of water whose waters do not fail."

Wow! If we can just get outside of ourselves and into others, we will be By taking care of the needs of others, we will be nourish our own spirit! Those are awesome promises! When we begin to speak blessings to others from a sincere heart, blessings begin to flow toward us.

Take the DE-out of Deprivation and live an "essential" filed life.

Chapter Twenty-Two: DE-PROGRAM

release (someone) from apparent brainwashing, typically that of a religious cult, by the systematic re-indoctrination of conventional values.

Conventional medicine doesn't always work. In this modern day, we have seen a rise in Depression, accompanied by a disturbing increase in ads for anti-depressants. Have you noticed the number of ads on TV that make claims that you need to add yet another medication, if your anti-depressant isn't working anymore. With the rise in medication use, there is a rise in cost to treat Depression. When my symptoms were not lifting, I consulted with my physician, and another medication was added. My symptoms actually worsened, and a start having involuntary muscle twitches which caused me to bite my tongue.

This is known as Tardive Dynkinesia. I decided I had, had enough. My symptoms were not being relieved. So, I decided to stop with medications. I needed my body to be deprogrammed and detoxed and that meant conducting my own self-study. I'm not advocating this for anyone that has not determined that you could handle the potential withdrawals or back lash from the abrupt cessation.. The worse side affect that I experienced was sleep disruption.

I have determined I would rather use natural alternatives to sleep. I also, added yoga as a means of relaxation and meditation. Timing my practice and exercise has helped immensely. While this might not work for everyone, I was willing to make the decision for my own mental health and wellness to endure some uncomfortableness. Deprogramming our bodies and our mind means we have to be willing to put behind us those things that haven't benefited us. We have to be willing to break some old habits, and thought processes and re-place them….REprogram.

The scripture refers to this as renewing of our minds. I believe it took leaving behind medications, practices, habits and adding new things, such as alternatives to drugs. These are the scriptures that I believe apply to De=pro-gramming to reprogram our mind, body, and spirit.

Romans 12:2 **Do not conform any longer to the pattern of this world, but be transformed by the renewing of your mind.** Then you will be able to test and approve what God's will is—his good, pleasing and perfect will.

Our religious upbringing can sometimes be a bigger hindrance than help. Many doctrines are that of 'hell, fire and brimstone", instead of grace and for-giveness. God does not intend for us to live with a "spirit of fear", some would consider this depression. **2 Timothy 1:7** - For God hath not given us the spirit of fear; but of power, and of love, and of a sound mind.

Take the De-out of Deprogramed and Reprogram your mind for a grace filled life.

Chapter Twenty-Three: DE-RAILED

1) (of a train or trolley car) accidentally leave the tracks.

2) obstruct (a process) by diverting it from its intended course.

There are times and going to be times that everything may be moving along smoothly. Then we encounter a problem that totally derails us. I spoke of a car accident in the previous chapter, which detoured me for a period of time....... when in reflection it could have totally De-railed me. When a train gets de-railed, it isn't a minor event. It's a "train-wreck"! Usually requiring a whole crew and heavy equipment to get it "back on track". It was probably rolling down the track, with an itinerary, on time, and a log appears in its path and it can't stop fast enough. There was no avoiding the inevitable. Brace yourself!

In my case, things really could have been worse! Yes, things can always be worse than they are.......I had a partial head-on collision, but by a split second later, I would have been t-boned and killed. The car that struck me was moving at 55 m.p.h., I was traveling at approximately 35 m.p.h.......combined collision forces were 90 m.p.h.! My life was spared. It took 6 months to get my train "back on track", but I did go back and finish my Master's degree in Exercise Physiology.

I believe the head trauma I experienced might have precluded some of my Depression, but I have never had a PET scan to see. De-railments occur when we remain inflexible to change. Yes, change. Our plans are not always God plan for us. Our timing may not be God's timing. I've been listening to Joyce Meyer, talk about being willing to change. Seek ye first the kingdom of GOD, and his righteousness, and all these things will be added unto you. *Matthew 6:33* What man has intended for evil, GOD can turn into GOOD.

Genesis 50:20 Joseph recognized this when his brothers had sold him into slavery, and Potipher's wife accused him falsely and he spent 9 years in prison. Ultimately, Joseph was promoted to a position of power and great respect.

A car accident that could have killed me, created a Determination in me to finish the "race", earn my degree, and not only finish but finish, STRONG! Philippines 3: 13-14, Press toward the mark, for the prize of the high calling of God in Christ. You too can overcome the Detours and derailments that life may have thrown your way. Everyday set your mind toward the "Prize".

All of us have different goals, dreams, aspirations in life. Don't let Depression, be terminal. Determine for yourself today, that your mindset and feelings can change. Improve your talk, to improve your walk. Though the medical community might differ philosophically, I believe Depression has a Mental, Physiological and *Spiritual* component. In order to overcome, the enemy, I Determined to declare war on it, mentally, physically, and spiritually. Let me explain further in Chapter 34, Determination.

Chapter Twenty-Four: DE-SENSITIZATION

1. having been made less sensitive.
"desensitized taste buds"
2. having been made less likely to feel shock or distress at scenes
of cruelty or suffering by overexposure to such images.

In psychology, desensitization is **a treatment or process that diminishes emotional responsiveness to a negative, aversive or positive stimulus** after repeated exposure to it. We all have had to address some **sensitive** issues and matters in life. From talking to a friend, or spouse, or our children about "the birds and the bees" to political discussions....and more.

Some events we encounter can leave us "traumatized". Even though this subject may seem off course, it ties into the effects that Depression can also have on your ability to handle situations with grace and poise. Depression is often coupled with other mental illness.

In my case, PTSD was the coupling illness. Symptoms that accompany PTSD are sleep disturbances, hyper-vigilance (quick to respond), and usually high levels of anxiety, and "depressed mood". I recommend that if you are having any of the symptoms mentioned that you seek medical diagnosis, as is the case with Depression.

Please do not try to "self-diagnose" in any psychiatric evaluation. Treatments vary.

I have suggested that this book is written with many personal experiences, as a testimony, to others that a healing is possible. So begins my journey with PTSD, and DE-sensitization training.

A soft answer turns away wraft...Proverbs 15: 1 "A soft word turn away wrath, but a harsh word stirs up anger". When put to the test...learn to respond rather react. I speak to this in my chapter on Decide and Desperate... When we can prepare by "role playing", have foresight rather than hind sight, we can live in a sphere of respect rather than regret!

De-sensitization training should involve a licensed mental health provider trained and experienced in trauma therapies. Become sensitive to your needs and be proactive!

Chapter Twenty-Five: DE-SERVE

do something or have or show qualities worthy of (reward or punishment).
Similar: be worthy of, be entitled to, have a right to, be qualified for, be good enough for

How many of us haven't felt we "deserved" something? to be loved? to be treated better? or Deserved a better life? or Deserved a second chance? or felt entitled to the parking space that someone else raced to get? or —————-
fill in the blank. Or "I don't deserve this", if someone was treated with disrespect or harshly.....maybe a parent disciplined your harshly? Maybe you were told you didn't "deserve" something. Can anyone relate to any of these examples? This attitude leads to a spirit of "entitlement". We live in a society that quite frankly encourages a spirit of "entitlement". I'm about to share some statistics that are quite staggering.

In total, Americans paid down **$110 billion** in credit card debt since the first quarter of 2020, an average of $2,049 per household. Mortgages fuel total debt. The average American holds $53,897 in personal debt, much of it tied up in mortgages. If mortgages are excluded, the average debt would drop to $16,720. Another source provided numbers from the pandemic.

Average household debt increased. The average household debt increased by 3.3 percent since the start of the pandemic to $155,038. More than three-fourths of all American households hold some form of debt. Credit cards are the most common type of debt, followed by mortgages and car loans. Nearly half of households have credit card debt, 40 percent have mortgage debt and 37 percent have car loans. Thirty-five percent of people reported being *stressed* by credit card debt.

We create our own stress that can be accompanied by Depression, as commonly a spirit of despair accompanies, long-standing inability to pay off a debt (with the exception of a mortgage as it is commonly deemed as a necessity). During the Pandemic housing sales were up by 30% in many areas, and debt rose to 30% as well.

I'm not saying this as a judgment.....I've been there. The debt cycle that seems never ending is incredibly discouraging and defeating. Yes, ultimately it can lead to Despair and Depression. So what can we do to prevent ourselves from getting caught up in this cycle of Debt. Spend less and serve more. Take the De-out of Deserve and Serve more. Become more service minded. Serve others, instead of serving our impulses and desires.

The practice of serving others and filling the need of others instead of filling our own desires accomplishes two things. It creates a more conscientious society in general and it helps others less privileged. While going through a divorce in 2020, I committed to "need-based" spending. If I didn't need it, I didn't buy it. I was left with some credit card debt from a failed marriage, and wasn't going to recover from it as long as I continued with my spending habits. The stress that over-spending creates was very apparent in our marriage. It contributed to the divorce. Financial stress is the primary cause of the majority of divorces. How can this attitude of Deserving and entitlement be remedied? Live with less. Simply don't go shopping unless you absolutely need what it is you're shopping for. Turn the "I Deserve" mentality into, I'll serve mentality.

[30] Love the Lord your God with all your heart and with all your soul and with all your mind and with all your strength.'[a] [31] The second is this: 'Love your neighbor as yourself.'[b] There is no commandment greater than these." Mark 12: 30-31

When we serve others, in essence we are demonstrating the love that is spoken of in the scripture above. The article I referred to earlier lists 10 ways to "Love your neighbor", means: 1) Receiving God's Love, 2) Loving ourselves as well, 3) Showing grace, 4) Acting with compassion, 5) Looking out for their well-being, 6) **Serving** them, 7) Speaking kindly to them, 8) making allowances for other people's humanity, 9) sharing in their joys and sorrows, and 10) Forgiving.

SERVING

Over the holidays this year, I was made aware of a friend of mine in Nashville, TN that had been arrested. The circumstances that brought about her mental state were brought about by the stress of excessive debt. In the years that I had known her, she had shared that her debt was insurmountable. She resorted to trying to make more money, rather than spending less. I had tried to encourage her to get some counseling for years, to potentially hire a financial manager. She persisted in her lifestyle.

Knowing that she had no family members living, tugged at my heart. I prayed about what I should do and spoke to my pastor. She needed help and I was available to help. I took the trip to Nashville, 9 hours from where I was living in Florida, to see if I could be of assistance. I did what I knew to do, and sent her phone money and commissary. I believed I was called to service. The situation was not resolved while I was there, but I'm sure she was comforted with the knowledge that someone out there cared. Acquiring a heart of service, instead of overspending for Christmas, lifted my spirits during a time that I ordinarily might experience deep feelings of seasonal depression.

I'm not going to sit here and tell you that I have conquered the debt monster. But I've made strides and it started with a commitment to stop unnecessary spending, and work on paying off current debts. I also started giving more to others, my time and resources, even giving to total strangers as called to do so. The practice of giving and serving, brings us a spirit of enlightenment. Blessing others, blesses us. It does a heart good. A merry heart doeth good like medicine. *Proverbs 17: 22*

There are many ways we can SERVE. We can volunteer with organizations in our community. We check in on elderly neighbors. We can lend childcare to someone, when there is a need. We can find a need for service in our church and fill it. We can give money or food to someone on the street. Look for a way to serve and see how it does your heart good. We were not put on this earth to serve ourselves. Serving others also, helps alleviate loneliness if you struggle with feeling lonely.

I came across an article on what it means to "Love our Neighbor as Ourselves" on line, Crosswalk.com. These are sincere acts that require we know how to love ourselves, not in a self-indulgent way, but in the way that GOD instructs us to love ourselves, as we are made in his image. He is a GOD of love. To serve him, is to love him. To serve others is to love ourselves, GOD and others. It's the nature of Service, if done with the proper motive, out of love.

In the story about the Prodigal son, he demonstrates a spirit of entitlement, but when convicted of his wrongful attitude is transformed. You can find the story in Luke 15. In *Luke 15: 12* The Prodigal son say "Give me my share!" But in, *Luke 15: 19*, When He returns and says, "Make me a servant". When your heart moves from self-centeredness to God-centeredness, you have moved to a service-centered life.

In a recent podcast, Pastor Rick Warren, author of "The Purpose Driven Life" described the process as 1) Getting fed up, 2) Own up, then 3) Offer up. The transformation takes time. Making the decision that starts the process. Getting "fed up" includes getting rid of the attitude of entitlement. It is by his grace that we are saved. Getting "fed up" includes being sick and tired of being "sick and tired", I'm describing Depression.

"Owning up", is determining where you are responsible for your own health and well-being. "Owning up", includes determining, the hurts, habits, and hang-ups, the sins, that we need forgiven.

Offer up. Offer yourselves as a living sacrifice, then "all these things will be added unto you." Offer up. God wants to give us the desires of our hearts, but it doesn't come without sacrifice. To get those things that we desire, we need to align our desires with his desires, Then see what the father's response was when the Prodigal came home, *Luke 15:23*. "Let us feast and celebrate."

Let's all learn to serve others better, by taking the De-out of Deserve and develop a Service-minded heart!

Chapter Twenty-Six: DE-SIRE

1. **strong feeling of wanting to have something or wishing for something to happen**
2. **strongly wish for or want (something)**
Similar: wish, want, fancy, inclination, aspiration, impulse, preference

DESIRE... lights the FIRE!

Delight yourself in the LORD and he will give you the **desires** of your heart.
Psalms 37;4

Someone with Depression losses their desires. It can impact every aspect of your life. Desire to have relationships is gone, Enjoyment is gone. Even your desire to live can be diminished by Depression. The devil comes to steal, kill and destroy.....he destroys our desire. One way to get your desire back, is to Delight yourself in the LORD!

Throughout this book, I've used DE-words to enlighten my reader about Depression from a spiritual perspective. Some words were easily changed to a positive. Let's take the DE-out of DEsire and see what remains......SIRE. Who is the SIRE of your life. GOD is often referred to as "Heavenly Father". He breathed life into man. Then he formed woman. He is responsible for our very existence, our very breath of life. When we place our dependence, our needs, and delight in him, he promises to give us the desires of our hearts. No one should desire to live a Depressed life. Desire lights the FIRE. Our passion for life is founded in our heartfelt desires. God wants to give us the desires of our heart. But, God requires something of us. He is our Heavenly sire. He designed, created and breathed the first breath of life into us. He wants to be the Sire of our lives.

The first commandment is "Thou shall love the LORD your GOD with all your heart and "love your neighbor as yourself" (The first and third commandments). If you truly desire to be free from Depression, developing a spirit-filled life that honors GOD will set you on the path of recovery and victory. I'm not saying that you might not need some form of medical assistance if your Depression is severe, and has gone untreated. God is the great healer, but I also believe that he equips medical professional that honor him to serve in the capacity as mental health practitioners. The process of healing from Depression, should be viewed from a holistic approach for best results.....a team approach that includes mind, body and spirit.

Your desire to be healed, should be guided by prayer and supplication. God guided me to the right physicians and mental health counselors when my Depression was at its most severe. I believe God ultimately directed my path to the right professionals to help, but I still had not addressed the spiritual component. Submitting to what God's will was for your life, included writing this book and sharing experiences, and perspectives in the process of healing.

This scripture alone conveys GOD's desire for us. 2 Timothy 1;7, "For I have not given you a **spirit of fear**, but of power, and love, and of **sound mind"**.

Let GOD's desire should be your desires... and let GOD sire your way out of Depression!

Chapter Twenty-Seven: DE-SPAIR

the complete loss or absence of hope.
synonyms: hopelessness, disheartenment, discouragement, desperation, distress, anguish, unhappiness; More despondency, depression, disconsolateness, melancholy, misery, wretchedness; defeatism, pessimism
"let me help you during this time of your despair"
antonyms: hope, joy
2. lose or be without hope.
synonyms: lose hope, abandon hope, give up, lose heart, lose faith, be discouraged, be despondent, be demoralized, resign oneself;

News Flash: How could such a capable human being, be in such a state of despair? I sat listening to the story of a young woman who had just had a baby 12 days earlier. She was found in the bathtub drowned. Shocking, you say. Sad. Unbelievable. Yes, and true. I was told that there was no cause of death determined in the autopsy, but there is no other explanation. She committed the unthinkable act of suicide. There is no other explanation. It just didn't add up. She had been a successful athlete, intelligent, newly married and started a family. Something just didn't add up. She must have been in complete despair.

And obviously depressed. But no one saw it in time. And it only took a moment, to take a life. It was a permanent solution, to a temporary state of mind.

I'm convinced that when someone reaches the state of actually committing the act of suicide, they really can't see another way out! This is one of the most difficult things I'm going to admit to you in the midst of writing this book, but I've been there. I can earnestly tell you what goes into the thought processes of wanting to end one's own life and.... what has prevented me from doing so. But I can't earnestly tell you how to prevent someone else from doing it. If they are determined to do it; they will. Suicide for some, is like a fox caught in a trap......that level of pain. A fox will literally chew their own leg off to ease the pain. Despair......Take the de- out of despair...... it leaves us spare.

God spared us of a lot of pain and suffering by allowing his very own son to take our place on the cross. for our sins......... GOD spares us, just as his "Eye is on the Sparrow." By sparing us, he's allowed us an opportunity for forgiveness, and correction. An opportunity for change...... This acrostic might help you if you have moment of Despair.

C......Cherish Joy

H.....Hope in the LORD

A....Always give Thanks

N....Never give up, Always keep trying

G....Give credit to all who help Journey.

E....Endlessly Endeavor to be a child of GOD.

This was contributed by my friend Pam McFadden, from La Follette, TN.

The key is realizing where that person is in the process and doing everything you can to bring prospective to the situation. A person has to grow to realize they are valuable, they have purpose, and they need to be able to have a safety net, a safe place to go, physically and emotionally, when the thoughts are fleeting through their mind. No one could begin to know the level of desperation that causes a human to be in that place, if they haven't ever been there in their own minds. Its hard to fathom.......but I am willing to share what lead to mine and how I keep myself from going into that mindset and ever committing such an unthinkable act.

My story:

I can't say it was any one thing that lead me to the place, or thoughts of wanting to end my own life. I just know the emotional burden was so heavy, so exhausting, and so Depressing that I couldn't imagine taking another step through life. My body even ached and felt so exhausted from the weight of it all that there were days I couldn't get out of bed except to go to the bathroom or get something to drink.

There were nights that I would wake up with thoughts of " this just can't go on". I had gone a year and a half without adequate employment. My debts had accumulated to the point where I couldn't keep up the payments on anything; credit card debtors were calling, my mortgage holder was calling, my car payment was late and I had moved to another state to take a job that didn't materialize. I was literally homeless, living in a storage facility that I had moved all of my earthly possessions into. It was 28 degrees in Nashville, TN, and this was my life. With my loyal dog, Lucy, resting comfortably beside me, I was able to fall asleep buried under the comforter and two other blankets as I climbed up into my bed in storage. What had brought me to this place? It's a long story.

I had two mortgages that I had taken on while employed as a school teacher. I had intended to start building my retirement portfolio with rental properties. Then I lost the teaching job.....it wasn't the first......I had experienced quite a few losses since reporting a former supervisor for sexual harassment and an employer for retaliating against me for reporting. There is no way to describe the way my "American Dream" turned into my "American Nightmare", but as I am here writing this, I realize that is exactly what had happened and lead me down a long trail of deep despair.

I'm not sure what makes a human being "crack", but the level of overload that and was experiencing surely would have been enough to make the average person feel overwhelmed, if not suicidal. Where do you find hope, in a hopeless situation? You have to look outside of the situation. You have to believe there is a better day ahead. You have to look beyond the pain and suffering. Sometimes you have to look back.....by that I mean, remember why you started..... remember what your level of commitment was before the storm. And remember what was and still is important in your life. That usually involves other people....family and friends.

I had delivered 3 children in natural child birthing experiences. I can honestly tell you I know the depth of physical pain. But to explain the level of emotional or psychological pain that I would endure in just unfathomable. Loss after loss. Please don't take this as a pity party, it is not intended to be, rather an acknowledgment of events that lead to the spiral and thought processes. There's really no logic or reason to all of it. When it started spiraling, it kept spiraling. Its what I describe as a paradox of Depression. You don't know if your depressed and it causes you to lose sleep or if losing sleep causes you to become depressed. One feeds the other, a cycle that can be very difficult to break without the assistance of professional help, albeit, the assistance of a physician who really listens and cares, or a licensed mental health practitioner who you trust. Reach out to a friend, or your pastor.

I tried to unload as much of the financial burden as I could but, just couldn't fast enough. I just looked up Bankruptcy to see if I could figure out what to do next with my financial situation. I've been contemplating it for a couple of years now.....but was told by an attorney that I wouldn't qualify as long as I held property. Now the property is so underwater, maybe it's time to reconsider. When we are under "maximum" stress load, it is time to reconsider what is truly important. We might need to unload some of the stressors, any of them that can be unloaded, that is.

This world system called the mortgage industry is really badly and sadly broken. I've experienced it first hand. The inability of not being able to pay debts is a weighty issue. For some, it seems not to bother them. But, for others, like myself, it is an incredible burden. Last year, I chose to eliminate all of my credit cards, except for one (for emergencies), in an effort to reduce the likelihood of bankruptcy. It raised the question of which is worst: emotional or financial bankruptcy....?

Ok, you have a glimpse of what was going on in my life that could lead to thoughts of suicide. But, that's not all. I developed a sense of worthlessness through job loss, coupled with feelings like "no one cares" immediate family, with the exception of my eldest daughter seemingly alienated me. I developed feelings of loneliness that didn't seem to go away. The kind that prevailed even when in a crowd or with someone else. Feelings of abandonment by your best of friends and family. Really? How could one endure all of this....but wait. That's not all......... Top it off with the loss of another job and housing situation. It's the sense of being a rat in a maze with four walls and all you do is keep bumping your head against the walls, can't find your way out. No way I ever thought I'd find myself in such a mess, as one of the chapters is named, a Debacle.

You've heard the phrase, "Rome wasn't built in a day", well neither was the debt well I was in, nor the employment situation, or the loneliness. It was through a series of events that derived a reputation and sense of lost self-worth. Yet another loss. One can't keep losing their way, and think you can maintain direction in life, can you? Who says you can't.......A ship can get blown off course time and time again and still make it to shore or its final destination.

Who's your captain? I once said, that the people employed to cut away at my reputation as a teacher in a lawsuit didn't know who I am or "whose I am". By that I mean, the God above me, must know and love me, or he wouldn't have put me on this planet in the first place. As useless as I feel somedays, I know that doing the little things can help me feel useful. Encouraging someone else can encourage me. Blessing someone else, blesses you!

And getting out and taking a long walk and breathing deep and looking at nature has a way of restoring some level of equilibrium in a situation that is so out of balance it might make one want to end it all. Be encouraged. If you never read the bible. Let me share some scriptures without sounding to overt. These have always helped me find some hope in a hopeless situation.

Philippines 4:13 I can do all things through Christ who strengthens me......
Isaiah 55:12 Go out in joy and be led forth in peace......

Deuteronomy 28:13 The LORD will open the heavens, the storehouse of his bounty, to send rain on your land in season and to bless all the work of your hands.

I can't take credit for knowing these scriptures as they were shared by and through a T.V. Ministry of Nicole and David Crank, pastors of Faith Church in St. Louis, Missouri. You can find them online and request free of charge a CD of positive declarations. At the time, I attended Faith Church in West Palm Beach, as they are launching a ministry there. I also volunteer my time in the nursery, "to bless and be blessed". Let me share a few more scriptures. So when you have moments of Despair....take the DE-out of despair and RE-pair your spirit.......

Isaiah 54:17 No weapon formed against you shall prosper, And every tongue which rises against you in judgment You shall condemn. In other words rebuke.

You have to believe that better days are ahead........we have been given an opportunity to live a better life a day at a time.... My eldest daughter attended a Suicide prevention workshop from which she received a book, "Suicide, The Forever Decision" by Paul G. Quinnett. I appreciate the tough questions he poses in the book. As I read each chapter, it felt like I was in a therapy session, with myself. Isn't that where this all originates with ourselves. In the state of mind that precedes the moments of suicidal thinking, there could be any number of things that triggers this thought process. He takes into account many of them: maximum stress, Anger, Depression, Hopelessness, Drugs/Booze, and Fatal mistakes, feelings of loneliness and lack of love.

I highly recommend reading, but be ready to answer some of these questions for yourself and possibly seeking the guidance of a trained professional mental health counselor, if needed. You might be thinking or saying, "Wait a minute!?".....If I'm thinking about committing suicide, do I really have time to read a book? Step away for a moment, find someone or something that means something to you, and ask if Suicide is the solution? I've shared a small piece of the picture that went into my own suicidal thoughts. Now it's time for you to share yours. Get personal, pour your heart out, let it all go.....write it down. Whatever it takes to prevent you from taking a permanent action to a temporary thought process! It's truly not the answer to whatever the level of despair you may be experiencing at this time.

"His Eye is on the Sparrow", Google search this one......Lauryn Hill and Tanya Blount. Almost 12, 000,000 hits. You are not alone, in your quest for peace, happiness or the assurance that someone cares.......He does! Matthew 10:31 "He has numbered the hairs on your head." I coined a phrase for my children, as I've gone through some of the adversities I spoke of....."If I had to go through this so that I could better instruct you through a tough time, then it has been worth it"......... I mean that.....God uses each one of us for a distinct purpose....and this may have been one of his intentions. As tough as it is for me to be saying this....as humbled as I feel to be in the place that I am in.......I want to encourage you to seek his help when no one else is there in your time of need.

How do we go from Despair to Repair ? This is going to be a silly analogy but it's all I have right now.......Have you ever had a flat tire? If so, I doubt you persisted in trying to roll around on it. If so, you didn't get very far......Having Depression and feelings of Despair is very much like riding on a flat tire. It's more difficult to get where you want to go.....sometimes you stop in your tracks...can't go any further until the tire gets repaired.....or replaced. If you never ask for help before, now is the time. Change that flat tire, get some air......

This may be the case for you....it was for me......total replacement...... a heart transplant had to occur.....I sing because I'm happy and I'm free...! His eye is on this sparrow..........who may have had a broken wing, but eventually that wing will heal and it will be time to take flight. Very much like a recovering alcoholic, a recovering depressive must take things in their own time. Be gentle on yourself. Time heals..............

Take the De out of Despair....Remember GOD doesn't spare His love, He gives it freely and abundantly. You are His by your chosing! Ask Him in today!

Chapter Twenty-Eight: DE-SPERATE

1. reckless or dangerous because of despair or urgency: a desperate killer.

2. having an urgent need, desire, etc.: desperate for attention.

3. leaving little or no hope; very serious or dangerous: a desperate illness.

4. extremely bad; intolerable or shocking: clothes in desperate taste.

5. extreme or excessive

Similar: hopeless, anguished, distressed, suicidal, last-ditch, last-chance, last-resort, last-minute

The above definition of Desperate was my favorite one that I located while doing a "Google" search for the definition of De-sperate. Primarily, because of the way the author chose to expand on the definition from one context to another.

1. reckless or dangerous because of despair or urgency: a desperate killer.

Have you ever been in a desperate situation? Felt like you were in a maze? in Danger?

Did you want to quit? Or fight your way out? If you haven't been, you will have been before life ends, as you know it. Even a toddler knows what desperate is when they reach before they fall to the ground from their first steps...they would grab anything within reach to avoid the inevitable...bump on the rump. Ouch! But it doesn't keep them from trying again.

Definition #1....2. having an urgent need, desire, etc.: desperate for attention. If you've ever been out, had too much water or coffee or your beverage of choice, and look around at the first urge to relieve yourself from the swelling feeling inside, to find that the closest restroom is at the end of the mall corridor.....you've been des·per·ate.

Definition #2.....
3. leaving little or no hope; very serious or dangerous: a desperate illness.

Those of you out there that have experience the abrupt feeling when your physician stands before you or the nurse has called to tell you they need to do further testing, it doesn't look good. Only to find out after the biopsy that it's the "C" word. Yes, Cancer, know the need for a rapid course of treatment. You might have even started your bucket list of things to do before the inevitable....as was once thought, terminal. But, if your reading this you know those feelings have subsided.

Definition #3....
4. extremely bad; intolerable or shocking: clothes in desperate taste.

I have to laugh out loud on this one...... The only example that comes to mind is one of those "Most Embarrassing Moments".....You get of from a park bench only to find that the person before you didn't wipe up the mess of ketchup from the hotdog they ate while watching the passers-by...... Yikes. Run and hide and go find some new pants......and they were white!

Definition #4.
5. extreme or excessive

Watching the Super Bowl several years ago, Seattle Seahawks and Denver Broncos..... the best of the best NFL! But,, oh, NO! Quarterback rush, players scramble, crunch he gets hit. The ball is released into the air, suspended for seconds.....The quarterback turns in a desperate.....he miscalculated the release in a desperate moment, under extreme pressure from the defensive line. It falls into the hands of the opposition.......interception! This is not looking good.

Definition #5.
By the way, the Quarterback I was speaking of was Peyton Manning. a SUPER BOWL champion. Did any of the descriptions of desperation hit home with anyone? Maybe make you laugh, winch. Or reflect on your own personal experience. Well, let's take this into the context of Depression.

When a person is dealing with depression, they can find themselves at some point in time Desperate for relief from the feelings that misalign their mind, body and spirit. This book is coming from a tremendously personal place at times, so bare with me, it is not my intention to cause more pain for anyone suffering in a depressed state, but rather to help you avoid making some of the most common mistakes, some causing irreparable harm to oneself or others.

When in a Desperate place, people will tend to make Desperate decisions. Many times thinking it will relieve the immediate circumstances or feelings, only to find that it compounds their condition. If this is true for you, then you know it can only add to the state of despair and depression, even move into self-loathing for making the mistake.

Be gentle on yourself.....try to avoid making decisions on your own until you feel less desperate. Trust a close friend or family member to assist in the decision making process. Trust that they have your back. One of the common symptoms of depression is confusion, indecisiveness, or foggy thinking. You might not be able to depend on those processes that once came so easily for you. It's alright to ask for help at these times. It's always Okay to "run something by" another person to check yourself without feeling helpless or dependent. It's better to be safe than sorry, my mother used to say.

Can you imagine for a moment how desperate Moses must have felt to get out of his uncomfortable situation when crossing the Red Sea? The Egyptians closing in behind him? The Sea raging on both sides trusting that it wouldn't close until he got to the other side. Look ahead to the other side. When depression creeps in, and you find yourself feeling desperate, what ever the situation, look to the other side, the green side, the shore, whatever your target keep aim and focused!

Take a long walk and tell yourself this too shall pass......the more oxygen you can get to your brain the clearer your thinking will become. Meditate on good things. And pray. Don't despair.! I use this scripture in several chapters for good reason!2 Timothy 1:7

"GOD HAS NOT GIVEN US A SPIRIT OF FEAR", BUT OF POWER, AND OF LOVE, AND OF A SOUND MIND."

Take the DE- out of DEsperate, and separate your emotions from the situation. The less desperate you become the more rational your decision making will be.

If you're experiencing a state of Urgency, an "urgent matter", HOPELESSNESS, SHOCK, or EXTREME Panic. Don't act DEsperate.

Chapter Twenty-Nine: DE-STINY

1. the events that will necessarily happen to a particular person or thing in the future.
2. the hidden power believed to control what will happen in the future; fate.
"he believes in destiny"
Similar: future, fate, fortune

Many religions or faiths believe in the predestation of human life. What do you believe? Do we have a destiny or is everything left to fate? to Chance? ...... I believe GOD has an ultimate plan, and I don't believe it included anyone living a depressed life.

He gave us all gifts, special talents, that makes us unique from each other. He also gives us free will. Which means we are given the privilege to choose. I've heard it said. GOOD LUCK is when , timing meets opportunity. If we left everything to fate, we would be floating around on planet earth without any direction or purpose. I believe God has given us all purpose, and it's up to us to find his divine purpose for our lives. take the word DESTINY and expand on it.......we have Destination. Our life on planet earth is a journey through time. and if you believe in Christ......you are granted an eternal destination, a home in heaven.

To fulfill our destiny, we must make the right decisions and choices. Those choices include a life lived in accordance with the 10 commandments.....for good reason. If we live by them, we will have no regrets. When we live outside of those confines and live in sin, it opens us up to the consequences of sin. One of the Consequences of sin is a LOW spirit.

I believe that much of depression is based in living outside of god's good and perfect will for our lives.......and we become either suppressed, repressed or oppressed, which leads to Depression.

Ephesians 2:10 We are created in Christ Jesus, so that we can do the things which God has pre-planned.

Philippians 4:13 I can do all things through Christ who strengthens me…

We can be content in all situations when we know that God is ultimately in charge of the universe in which we live. Living in the capacity of Destiny includes living a happy, victorious life. outside of our circumstances. We all will experience trials and tribulations. We live on this planet meant for perfect harmony, but destroyed by man's own choices.

Let's stay focused on God's will for our lives, and our destiny and future will always be guided by his light. Our destiny includes learning when to be content. This is spoken of in Philippians 4:12, [12] I know what it is to be in need, and I know what it is to have plenty. I have learned the secret of being content in any and every situation, whether well fed or hungry, whether living in plenty or in want."

While we live out our destiny, we can learn to be content, and when this is accomplished.....there is no room in our lives for Depression.... our minds are set on a positive path because we know we serve a god who has our best interest at heart. For he know the plan he has for us. Jeremiah 29:11 "For I know the plans I have for you"........that comes with a promise. Take your place in God's plans and live out your destiny!

Chapter Thirty: DE-STROY

verb
1. put an end to the existence of (something) by damaging or attacking it
2.ruin (someone) emotionally or spiritually.
3. defeat (someone) utterly.
Similar: destruct, demolish, obliterate, wipe-out, annihilate ...
and the list goes on...

Disclaimer: This may be one of the "darkest" chapters of this book. Persevere with me through this as I share parts of my story that could be deeply disturbing, but necessary to shed light on how far into the "pit" depression can take a human being, and how to potentially rewrite your story if you suffer from depression. Depression goes beyond reasoning. It goes beyond the logical. It goes beyond the human spirit. Depression does not discriminate. Depression infiltrates the mind, brain, and body. Depression can be difficult to treat, because it can be multi-focal.

Depression can be specific or non-specific. It can come after an event, or very unsuspecting. Depression is deceptive, here one day and gone tomorrow (as in manic/depressive disorder, also known as Bipolar I and/or II). I don't believe we are born with "depression," but we can be born with the predisposition if there is a family history, very much like other diseases such as diabetes, heart disease, and high blood pressure.

Depression is uncertain and creates confusion. It can make us "feel" defeated.

Depression can make one question their very purpose in life and even their reason for existence. Depression is evil. It tries to *destroy* what life we have left in us. This all sounds negative and it is, but hang on! We are going to press on! Depression can *steal* our joy, our energy, our vision (literally and figuratively speaking.) It steals whatever it can from us. It is a thief in the day and night. Depression can *kill*. The end road to depression can be suicide. This is a very difficult subject to address, but I believe I can lend insight, and only because I was spared to tell my story. Depression can destroy. Every aspect of our lives, mental and physical health, wealth, relationships, ambition …

The thief does not come except to steal, kill and *destroy (John 10:10.)*

We can destroy the Destroyer … by taking the DE- out of destroy and turning it in our favor.

We can create our own STORY …

STORY: Creating your own recovery and success story!
Start with Awareness:
In order for someone to begin to understand their path to healing, they need to be aware of the clinical symptoms of depression. I detailed the symptoms in another chapter. Awareness is known to be the beginning of many 12-step recovery programs.

I have personally attended Celebrate Recovery, which focuses on Hurts, Habits, and Hang-ups and addresses any "dysfunction" a person desires to be healed from.

Teach or educate yourself:
My awareness of my own decline in mental health came about when I was teaching high school health. We were discussing a check list for depression symptoms as the mental health unit. I identified with every symptom on the list. It was time for the teacher to educate herself and to take action. You will find a list of resources at the end of this chapter which are educational.

<u>**O**rganize a treatment plan:</u>

This *will require* the assistance of health care professionals who have more insight into your particular symptoms and course of treatment. I am not a diagnostician or mental health professional. I have called upon literally every resource to implement an action plan for treatment of depression for a multifocal approach. I believe in the holistic approach, which incorporates mind, body, and spirit for whole wellness.

<u>**R**each out to others for support:</u>

Man was not intended to be an island to himself (or woman to herself.) When I was a personal trainer in my twenties, I was part of the support team for clients desiring to implement an exercise and nutritional program. Having a "buddy" for accountability and morale support increases the odds of success, and making a life style change.

The same approach can assist in combating depression, especially in your lowest hours or days.

Small group support groups are available and provide many options for attendance.

Inevitably, there will be an opportunity for you to "return the favor."

Suggested groups: Celebrate Recovery, CODA, AA, any church small group that meets an area of need in your life.

<u>**Y**earn for a healing:</u>

Yearning … having a deep **desire to** really, really want it. An urgent longing.

Desire lights the Fire.

"WHATEVER THE **MIND** OF MAN CAN CONCEIVE AND BELIEVE, IT CAN ACHIEVE" - Napoleon Hill

Part of my personal STORY is the acknowledgment and incorporation of the spiritual component of depression. Philosophically, this is unlike most schools of thought you might encounter in your quest for healing. I encourage you to research and ask questions, and seek any and all remedies available to you in your "war" on depression. I went through years of searching and tried traditional remedies, prescribed a plethora of medications, subscribed to talk therapy, and even periods of hospitalizations and intensive outpatient clinics. I do not discount any of the benefits of traditional remedies and management of depression. But I had a true yearning for a "healing."

As a matter of fact, in the first meeting of Psychiatrist Lucas Van Orden, he asked why I was in his office. While I went through the traditional intake interview, at the end he asked, "what do you want from this?" My response was simply, "I want to be healed of this." That was in 2003.For many years I cycled through periods of mild to deep depression, seemingly they followed several challenging life events, and losses. Some things and events bring on sadness, possibly grieving, but the type of depression I was suffering with lingered and infiltrated every area of life. In all of those years, I knew my spirit was in deep despair. I had to dig deeper to find the wound contributing to living in the state I was in. The more I dug out the "splinter," as I refer to in another chapter, the more complete my healing has become. Desire to live a full, productive life takes work, honesty, imploring others, and yes, I believe resting and relying on GOD.

God has given us "free will," which is managed by the mind. *Philippians 2:13* says, "For it is (not your strength, but it is) GOD who is effectively at work in you, both to will and to work (that is, strengthening, energizing, and creating in you the *longing* and the ability to fulfill your purpose)for his good pleasure. (cited from the Everyday Life Bible, Amplified version)

The Holy Spirit has the power to make the changes God wants to make in our lives. These two spirits are mingled together when we are born again, as we take on the character of Christ. Dr. Carolyn Leaf explains how to "rewire" the brain by changing the neurophysiology by taking time to do something pleasurable everyday. It takes time, desire, and an exercise

of the human will, which is divinely inspired when we call upon the Holy Spirit into our heart. We were "fearfully and wonderfully" made, but through life events and experiences, our minds can become dysregulated. Dr. Leaf is a Christian neurophysiologist who has earned the respect of the medical community and her peers. Her podcasts are a great resource for education. Joel Osteen is another powerful speaker with a positive, faith-filled message. This morning he was teaching from Zephaniah 3. The moment you pray, the tide of battle turns. Go to GOD in prayer, express your yearning (longing, craving, burning desire) to be healed. It is GOD's desire. He will give us the desires of our hearts (spirits) and help us take the DE- out of destroy, and write our own success STORY and victory against depression.

One of my favorite scriptures can be found in Isaiah, 40:31. "They that wait upon the LORD, he will renew your strength, you will mount up with wings as eagles, walk and not be weary, run and not faint."

It is my sincere desire this book moves you to a place of action, to seek your own healing so you can take the DE-out of Destroy and write your own success STORY!

These are some podcasts I found helpful in my quest for recovery and education.

Daily Hope by Rick Warren author of *Purpose Driven Life* and Pastor of Saddleback Church.

Joyce Meyer, author of *Battlefield of the Mind* and thirty other books addressing specific areas of struggle and practical life applications.

Celebrate Recovery, workbooks and learning guides.

Joel Osteen, Lakewood Baptist Church, Houston TX.

Dr. Caroline Leaf, Neurophysiologist, author of *Cleaning up Your Mental Mess*.

Anna Runkle of the *Crappy Childhood Fairy*, addresses issues with Complex Post-Traumatic Stress Disorder (CPTSD).

Chapter Thirty-One: DE-STRUCT

1. serving or designed to destroy:

2. the act or process of intentional destruction:.

Here, I want to focus on whether it's someone else committing the action or yourself that is at the helm of the ship, via self – destructive behavior, either can lead to depression or be a by-product of depression. Wow, wrap your mind around that one.

In some ways, I feel so inadequate to be writing such a book as this, at times overwhelmed by the daunting task, other times feeling completely in-adequate to fulfill what I know has been a calling to do so. I have been told that I have a creative mind and have learned to embrace that notion. But I keep in mind that I have a creator that enabled me to be here and it's by his design that I believe the concept for this book was birthed.

This chapter is meant to address the nature of how destructive our own thoughts can be, how destructive other peoples words or actions towards us can be, and ultimately, if we allow either to perpetuate, can lead to self-de-structive behavior. How do we turn it around? How can we make what has been destructive......constructive?

The enemy comes to steal, kill, and destroy......*John 10:10* We generally think of the enemy as being the devil, or someone other than our friends.

We are not free of false teachers today.....Peter wrote, "There will be false teachers among you." They will introduce destructive heresies, denying the sovereign Lord who made them, bringing swift destruction to themselves." *II Peter 2:1.*

The false teachers this passage speaks of can come in the form of friends, strangers, and even the little voices inside our minds, the demon voices that send destructive messages. The messages could range from self-deprecating comments, name-calling, feelings of self-doubt, insecurities, external and internal criticisms, which then lead to self-destructive behaviors.

Our Friends.....

"choose your friends wisely" Proverbs 1:10-19 How many of us would really choose friends that speak ill will against us.......many of us do. How many of us likes to be criticized or judged when we make mistakes? Our friends should be a source of encouragement.

"Encourage one another.. Thessalonians 5:11, and build each other up."

Many times we allow other people around us to determine who we are by what they say about us; but true friends are ones that "build us UP"! So, if you are around the kind of friends that would prefer to criticize than complement., it's time you found a new social group.....

This is much easier said than done when you struggle with depression.

Depression tends to limit your mindset of social involvements. I do recommend finding friends with common hobbies and interests, things that bring joy to your life. Friends.com....it's not that easy.

There are support groups that can meet this need. There are health and fitness facilities with people with healthy attitudes or those attempting to maintain healthy lifestyles.

Be willing to take on a new hobby, to create a new circle of friends. Isolation is also a by-product of someone who struggles with depression......you will only perpetuate the problem if you stay isolated too long.

Find a church home that meets your lifestyle needs. There are an array of inter-denominational, non-denominational, and denominational churches. Just sitting in church can make you feel more connected. If you haven't ever attended, you might want to start by viewing a television program such as the one I found when I moved to South Florida, FaithChurch.com. Based in St. Louis, Missouri, Faith Church has a weekly broadcast with life applicable messages. Further, when they recently satellited a church to West Palm Beach, Florida and announced they needed nursery workers, I got involved. Through viewing Pastor David and Nicole Crank, I became more convinced of making positive declarations to improve my negative thoughts and feelings about myself. That leads me to the next section on Self-destruction.

Self-Destruction...... I'm talking about drug use, alcohol abuse, ...suicide.

It's completely counter-productive to think that anyone would commit self-destructive acts or intentionally speak self-destructive things to ourselves, but it happens to us everyday. How many times have you thought, "that was stupid, stupid"......today? Over the most petty mistakes!

The things we say to ourselves and the voices we hear inside matter, as much or more as the voices we hear of others. What you think of yourself matters most.....or at least it should to you.

Author Debbie Ford, addresses "Why Good People Do Bad Things". I highly recommend her writings, as they encouraged me to reflect on things that had formed my ego and contribute to self-destructive behaviors thoughts and attitudes. I can't include much of what I learned in other people's writings, but I can give reference to one's that I found helpful in enlightening me upon my journey to be Delivered from Depression. My goal is to experience the symptoms of Depression less and less until I experience a Deliverance.

News break......July 11, 2014 My favorite evening game show was just interrupted with the shocking announcement of the death of Actor, Author, and comedian, Robin Williams. His comic relief brand of humor, spanned three generations. From Mork and Mindy, to talks about his latest film Ms. Doubtfire II, Robin was a supreme human being. But, something was broken. And he's not around now for us to ask what it was.......but I can estimate based on my own and other experiences I've heard in counseling sessions.......his heart and spirit were broken. He was in a state of total desperation, despair, despondency. Apparently, his death was confirmed by county coroner as asphyxia by hanging.

I don't want to even pretend to be a know-it-all. Depression is a very deceptive disease. Dr. Drew states, this is an illness. But this is where I can speak to the demons that enter your mind when the illness is raging untreated or out of control. Many brain disorders need additional brains to treat the disorder, to bring order to the disordered thinking. Reflection............

The master healer, God, or as AA, calls it, HIGHER POWER, has to be called upon to intercede in moments were this kind of despondency exists.......Love, Hopes in all things....God is love. The stigma of mental illness creates a very lonely existence. A person struggling on the edge of suicide is not safe with themselves, but may also lack feeling emotionally safe disclosing their struggles with someone else for fear of not being believed.......or in the case of Robin Williams for fear of being talked out of committing the act of suicide. Keep in mind suicide is a **permanent** solution, to a **temporary** problem...or mindset. I heard it said, that the victim is in a temporary state of psychosis. A state of mind that often precludes suicide.....where the victim losses touch with reality.

Take the DE- out of destruct and Construct a Plan for Healing today!

Chapter Thirty-Two: DE-TECT

1. to discover or catch (a person) in the performance of some act: to detect someone cheating.
2. to discover the existence of: to detect the odor of gas.
3...to find out the true character or activity of: to detect a spy

You may have heard this in regards to saving a life and the early "detection" of cancer. This can actually apply to any disease; that of the mind or body. In a previous chapter, I speak candidly about the discovery of my depression while delivering a lesson in my health classroom. The topic that day was emotional health and well-being. I contend many people who suffer from depression go a long time without reporting it, though they may experience symptoms much earlier. The initial response to many health issues is that of De-nial.... if we are going to intercept and potentially alleviate a problem, we must work to detect it earlier...... This applies to Depression.

I'm not advocating being over zealous either. We all go through periods of the occasional downs or blues. I'm talking about recognizing when it turns into an ongoing or habitual situation. Read the definition again. ....To discover, to find out.... With depression, it may take more than discovering to take action. I suggest you ask a close friend or family member if they have noticed anything different about the way you are acting or changes in your behavior, such as limiting your social outings or interactions. Identifying life events that can trigger depression is also helpful, such as loss of loved ones, or recent changings in work or other stressors. We live in a society of the over-achievers mentality and stress ourselves by taking on more than is humanly possible at times. This combined with a lack of sleep can contribute to lower serotonin levels in the brain. Because brain chemicals are not detectable in the blood stream, there is no way to know when they decline or are depleted except by the showing of symptoms. Much of the time symptoms are very pronounced before we address them in depression, giving way to an acute or chronic loss of quality of life.

I want to encourage you or if you know someone that is suffering from any of the signs to address the issue and be proactive; seek the assistance of a physician, psychiatrist (specialist in mental diseases or disorders), psychologist, or social worker, that can help you determine a course of treatment.

Signs and symptoms of depression may include any combination or all of the following:

1. Feelings of helplessness and hopelessness. ...
2. Loss of interest in daily activities. ...
3. Appetite or weight changes. ...
4. Sleep changes. ...
5. Anger or irritability. ...
6. Loss of energy. ...
7. Self-loathing. ...
8. Reckless behavior

The list above are the manifestations of Depression. These are the outward signs of the inner struggle.

From my experience, there is always an inner struggle or unmet resolved issue that underlies the Depression. By the time I reached out for help, through my general practitioner, I was in full blown Clinical Depression, manifesting all of the above. I keep reiterating that God does not want us to live with a "spirit of fear", but of "sound mind".

The Greek word for sound mind is sophronismos. It appears in the Bible only one time. 2 Timothy 1:7, was written by Paul when he was in prison. Imagine being in a physical prison, awaiting execution, and speaking of this very concept. Paul's letter to Timothy is filled with love and concern and encouragement, as Paul's impending execution would leave Timothy with the responsibility of leading the church and spreading the Gospel, the job the Paul had initiated.

In this message, we do not detect any Depression that Paul might have encountered being in the predicament that he was in, rather just the opposite. He acknowledges that God has not given us a "spirit of fear, but of "sound mine". Various translations describe sophronismos, as self-control, self-discipline, discipline, good judgment, and sound judgment. Paul is conveying this to Timothy to pass on the legacy of spreading the gospel and God's love.

The influence of the HOLY Spirit is required to produce a genuinely "sound mind". If you have detected any of the symptoms of Depression that I have described, or any others that may be specific to your personal experience, please take the time to inspect your personal spirit, and as a part of your journey to recovering and healing from this paradoxal disease. Take the Detection, and inspect yourself by doing a deep inventory of your life experiences that may have contributed to Depression. Depression can be rooted in a "spirit of fear". "For God has not given us a spirit of fear and timidity, but of power, love, and self-discipline."

The following are scriptures about courage. The courage that God wants to give us to face the enemy of Depression that robs us of life's joys and energy to serve him.

Deuteronomy 31:6 "Be strong and courageous. Do not be afraid or terrified because of them, for the Lord your God goes with you; he will never leave you not forsake you."

Joshua 1:6 "Be strong and courageous, because you will lead these people to inherit the land I swore to their ancestors to give them."

John 14:27 Peace I leave with you; my peace I give you. I do not give to you as the world gives. Do not let your hearts be troubled and do not be afraid.

1 Corinthians 16:13 Be on your guard; stand firm in the faith, be courageous, be strong.

Don't be afraid to Detect, and inspect, and move forward toward a healing from Depression!

Chapter Thirty-Three: DE-TERMINATION

1. firmness of purpose; resoluteness.
Similar: resolution, resolve, resoluteness, will power, strength of will, strength of character single-mindedness, sense of purpose, firmness of purpose, purposefulness, intentness, decidedness, steadfastness, perseverance, persistence, tenacity, tenaciousness, staying power strong-mindedness, backbone, the bulldog spirit, pertinacity, stubbornness, spiritedness, braveness, bravery, boldness, courage, courageousness, stout-heartedness, Dunkirk spirits itzfleisch, guts, spunk, grit, stick-to-it-iveness, intension, perseveration

Many of the words above are synonymous with determination. Take one (or more) and own it for yourself. Let me just say, in advance, this is what may have saved my life. Having a strong-willed determination. I believe I had a "decidedness" long before some events took place in my life. My mother used to say that I was "strong-willed", but not in the sense that I'm using it here, laugh out loud. Stubbornness, can keep us alive, or it can cost us our life.

I read a book by Victor Frankl, Austrian Neurologist, who survived the worst of the prison war camps during the Holocaust. What he describes is the "will" of man to survive in the most adverse conditions. His book, "Man's

Search for meaning" came highly recommended by my daughter, Amanda Alexander, PhD Psychologist. It's a short read and quite profound.

A process that requires forethought, resolve, intention. None of us intends to get Depression or be Depressed. It strikes when least desired or expected. It may linger for longer than anyone would estimate. I found that determining a daily course of action, is important. Depression can rob us of Desire, so we have to be intentional, if we want to overcome depressive thoughts. Even when depressed most of us can set small goals, and Determine to meet those goals.

Depression tends to impact one's desire. But with goal-setting, this isn't based on how we feel at any given moment. Goals are established based on what we believe is within the realm of possibility for ourselves. I've learned to set reasonable daily goals, mid-term goals, and long-term goals, and establish realistic time lines for obtaining those goals.

Without goals, we would be inclined to float aimlessly through life and when the least of events takes us off track, we might feel defeated. A Detour, or De rail, does not have to be a total Defeat! They might actually give us an opportunity for re-evaluation. reassessment, then refocus. I've learned to give myself more grace. Be kind to yourself. With Determination, an adverse life event, can actually be a springboard to a better future.

With Determination, a life event doesn't have to terminate our desire to achieve. When Depression, can take that peace away and fill us with self-doubt, we need to look to something, or someone, to help reaffirm and determine, that we weren't meant to live a Depressed life.

John 14:27 talks about Peace. "Peace I leave with you. My perfect peace I give to you. Do not let your heart be troubled, nor let it be afraid. Let my perfect peace calm you in every circumstance and give you courage and strength for every challenge.

Overcoming Depression can be a constant challenge. Many of the chapters in this book were written, to de-monstrate the negative connotation that "DE" has in our language and when removed can turn into a positive action. I would leave you with this thought. If you take the DE- out of Determination or DE-out of Determine, it leaves us with terminate. I would submit in order to terminate or overcome Depression, we need the DE- to build the Determination. It sounds contradictory. In this case, the DE- is the drive!

By no means am I trying to make it sound as easy as 1-2-3. But, when we resolve in our minds and spirits, that we are going to overcome, we lay the foundation to defeat any disease, albeit Physical or mental. Determination of spirit, Determination of will, with the JOY of the Lord as our strength, we can create a path to Defeat Depression, so that we can take the DE- out of Depression and PRESS ON! These verses are suggested for meditation.

Psalms 30 1-5

Sing praises to the LORD, O you his saints, and give thanks to his holy name.

For his anger is but for a moment, and his favor is for a lifetime. Weeping may tarry for the night, but Joy comes in the morning.

Ecclesiastes 9:11

The race is not to the swift, nor the battle to the strong, but to the one who holds out (stays determined).

Philippians 3:13-14

*Brethren, I count not myself to have apprehended: but this one thing I do, forgetting those things which are behind, and reaching forth unto those things which are before. 14.I **press** toward the mark for the prize of the high calling of God in Christ Jesus.*

Chapter Thirty-Four: DE-TOUR

noun

1. a long or roundabout route that is taken to avoid something or to visit somewhere along the way.

verb

2. take a long or roundabout route.

There's road block ahead! It appears they are trying to repair some part of the highway which has been damaged by the elements. Detour, it takes us out of the way, takes more time, lengthens our journey, and requires more patience. We don't often think of a detour as a minor inconvenience, because they usually come unexpected, which allows us little time to adjust our own agendas. We generally have to submit to "going with the flow," which is against our human nature.

Whether literally or figuratively, we all have experienced them in some form or another. The personal example I will use to illustrate occurred to me while I was attending Graduate school at Florida State University. After finishing my Undergraduate degree in Secondary Education, I decided to further my studies toward a Master's degree in Exercise Physiology with the encouragement of one of my undergraduate professors.

Life Event: While returning from a departmental party held on the Gulf Coast, I missed a stop sign and headed into the path of an oncoming car. Though the accident was life threatening, mine was spared. I had multiple injuries, which included an avulsion to my right eyelid, concussion, fractures in both of my arms, and my legs were slammed into the dash causing lacerations and trauma to the knees. I had an "out-of-body" experience and knew I was in another place for a brief period. When my traveling buddy, Barry, began to pull me from the car from my arms, I literally snapped out of it, crying in agony from the pain.

I hardly remember the ER, as I was in so much pain in so many different areas of my body, I eventually was sedated for surgery and woke up to the familiar faces of my parents, who had driven all night to be by my side. After three days of recovering at my grandfather's house in Georgia, I told my parents I was ready to continue with my studies. That was nearly laughable. If you could have seen me then, you would have understood instantly. I had a "mummy" wrap around my head and right eye, casts on both arms, and compression bandages on both knees. It was very unrealistic to think I could have handled the academic rigors of Graduate school as injured as I was. My parents insisted I withdraw and return to their home to mend.

DETOURED by the injuries, but not willing to give up on my dream of earning my Master's degree, I returned the next summer to continue my studies and ultimately completed my Master's degree in Exercise Physiology. The DETOUR gave me time to reflect, recover, and recharge. I returned even more determined to finish what I started and did with the encouragement of my parents. A DETOUR from our own agenda can either be a relapse in our thinking or a springboard to better things ahead.

By God's grace I experienced a full recovery from the injuries and have lived a productive life. The one thing that has kept me curious, though, as I have experienced depression, is whether or not the impact with the windshield and subsequent head injury, could have precluded the depression. It is well documented traumatic head injuries often result in postponed onset of depression. I have never been evaluated for brain injury with tests which could dispense of this curiosity or confirm my suspicions. A PET scan is the most current test which could detect any sign of remnants from the head injury, and it wasn't available at the time of the accident.

God will often give us a vision of our destiny long before we are prepared to actualize it.He did when he told Abraham there would be a 400-year detour in Egypt before they would reach their promised destination *(Gen. 15; 12-16)*.

Depression can set us off course from the destiny were intended to live. DE-tour: As it pertains to depression, the brain can take a brief detour from its customary performance when depression strikes. Your thinking might not be as sharp as usual. Decision-making becomes more of a challenge. It is not really clear to me when my first bout of depression occurred, but I do recall standing in front of a classroom while teaching high school health, going over amental health check list with students, when I realized I met every criteria for depression. That was a moment of awakening. I was telling my students if they had more than three of the symptoms, they should see the school counselor for further assessment.

I scheduled an appointment with my physician, to "practice what I was preaching." If your symptoms are severe, then the first course of treatment is usually to put a person on an antidepressant. The one thing I have always been committed to is exercising daily for physical and mental health. Within minutes of beginning exercise, even if just a simple walk around the block, there is a noticeable elevation in mood. Exercise also enhances the benefits of medication. If your life is on a Detour due to Depressive symptoms, take all measures to get back on course. The longer a person allows the condition to go untreated, the more difficult it is to dispense of.

It's hard to think of your life goals when you're depressed, but that's exactly what I recommend when you've taken a brief mental detour. Tour through picture albums and remind yourself of good times and look to a future of better times. Tour through your accomplishments. Tour through positive affirmations. Tour through scripture. Getting back on a path of positive thinking can help chase away the blues which accompany depressive episodes.

Meditation is a way to take a tour in your mind and release positive energy. Use scripture to get you back on track emotionally and spiritually.

Psalms 19:14, "Let the words of my mouth, and the meditation of my heart, be acceptable in thy sight, O LORD, my strength, and my redeemer".

Psalms 104:34, "My meditation of him shall be sweet; I will be glad in the LORD."

Take the DE- out of Detour and get back on track!

Chapter Thirty-Five: DE-VELOP

1. to bring out the capabilities or possibilities of; bring to a more advanced or effective state: to develop natural resources; to develop one's musical talent.
2. to cause to grow or expand: to develop one's muscles.
3.to elaborate or expand in detail:
Similar: grow, evolve, mature, expand, enlarge, spread, advance

All of us has had to develop our own sense of who we are.....from birth to whatever age you are, you have been developing and will continue to develop this sense of self. We can't just stop doing what we do as human beings, that is.....to be human. However, somewhere in your development, if trauma occurs, or there's a life altering event that could inhibit your normal growth and development, you could have been *detoured or detained* in the course of development.

I've committed to writing this book from a very vulnerable state, very personal place, but this is one that I'm still having difficulty with. I don't want to fabricate any of this, I want this to be very authentic, transparent, but in the same breath, I don't want to appear to know it all. So, please don't misconstrue these thoughts or perspectives, as expert opinion.

Debbie Ford's book "Why good People, do Bad things", helped me become reacquainted with the formation of ego. And that's where I'm coming from in this chapter, the development of ego, a sense of self, and self-worth.

I'd also attempt to address what to do when that sense is altered by life events out side of our control. How not to be shaken, when this occurs, and if you are shaken how to redevelop, reacquaint yourself and redirect your energies to formulate a positive and productive pathway for living without depression.

Depression can take us way of course. I speak to this in my chapter on Detour and Derailing.....

In a effort to get back on course, I found it helpful to develop strategies for daily living....

Some of these are going to sound incredibly simplistic. But when you're dealing with debilitating depression, the kind that has you captive under the covers, the negative voices whirling around inside your head and no one else around to encourage you, you need to have foresight and forethought in advance as to how you are going to manage those moments.

I started this chapter at midnight one night while tossing and turning. Sleep wasn't coming easily. I've thought I'd mastered the art of deep breathing.....Inhale on 4 count, Exhale on 4 count concentrate on the air moving in and moving out.....settle into a mantra.....just listening to your own breathing mechanics........It wasn't working. This is very much like centering your thoughts while doing Yoga practices.

Next strategy, get up and read or write....in this case write. So I began this chapter......

De- velop. My thoughts were racing......still too many stressors compounding my life. I had not developed any means for reducing stress in these times.....I simply had never expected to be in the situations I've found myself in.

So, if the strategies are not in place it's time to develop some......kind of like Map-questing a trip to know what route you should take to get there safely, on time. Even on Map-quest there are detours. I mentioned previously that depression is often coupled with anxiety. If you experience this, you are not alone....! Take a deep cleansing breath! Let it out slowly. Convert that nervous energy into something more productive.......even if it's housework! You may laugh at this suggestion, but at least utilizing the energy in a productive manner has two benefits.....you burn the energy and you get some of your housework done.......Take the trash out, while getting the trash out!.....Lol.

If it's sleeplessness you struggle with there is a method of relaxation called Tense and Relax. I have found this helpful at times.... This is done lying down. Follow a path from toe to head.......or head to toe.........Begin by tensing one body part, let's say your shoulders to your ears.... and release while exhaling.

Next tense your biceps (the muscles on the front of the upper arm)......and release while exhaling. Next tense your fist, as tight as you can........then release and let all of the tension go.....Now tighten everything from your shoulders to your fists.....now let it go.....! Breathe! This process is described in many stress management programs as Tense and Release. You can Google search find more.......Let's continue and do the whole body releasing tension from Head to Toe!

Now that's a strategy for relieving stress and hopefully getting you into a good night's sleep....If you should awaken in the middle of the night, these same strategies can be applied. Develop better eating habits. Exercise habits. Life-style habits.....Where do we begin? Today!

To Develop these habits, might involve reaching out to professionals in these particular disciplines. So much information is available to us by way of the internet and Podcasts. There are also, available professionals as Nutrition-ists, Exercise trainers at gyms, and life-coaching.at minimal costs. I've curtailed a lot of my expenses in podcasting but that may not work for everyone.

As I write this, I'm developing my daily strategy and schedule....for more enjoyment in the day... Remember to take some time out....everyday. Make room for peace and meditation.

In the womb, it takes us nine or ten-months from the point of conception to birth to develop enough of our organ systems to survive out of the womb. Of course, there are occasions where a baby is premature, but allowed the op-portunity to remain for the gestational duration, much better chance at a good start on life. Likewise if we develop healthy strategies, habits, life style, and thought patterns....we stand a far better chance of surviving adverse life events. There is no guarantee that we are going to be void of hardships in life. Without the TEST, we would have no TESTIMONY.

The common denominator here is we need to develop means to combat these life events in hopes of preventing further damage. Depressions can often develop when we are in a stressful situation, being tested beyond our means..... Some of these events include, loss of a loved one.... loss of a job, ...loss of a dream.......loss of a friend..... Loss of your identity in a relationship,

Loss of any kind can result in a period of low mood, when not dealt with can evolve into a major depressive episode. We are creatures of MIND, BODY, and SPIRIT, so an attack on any of those components can leave us more vulnerable to depression.

Personal story: When my father passed away in 2012, I lost 10 lbs. in two weeks. While some might welcome that weight loss, I couldn't really afford it. An unusual Weight loss or gain, such as what I experienced, is symptomatic of Depression. I already had the propensity to experience Depressed mood, but his unexpected lost caused me to mourn and grieve more deeply than I truly anticipated. I had not resolved some matters with him and consequently was not able to "say good-bye" before he passed unexpectedly.

I had to develop new strategies to deal with his loss. One strategy I used, was to visit his grave side and have a "final" talk. It worked for me. Sometimes when the person that you may have a grievance with is no longer available to confront, you might seek resolution by whatever means are available. Grief therapy is another option.

I also, developed a "daily practice" which some call journaling. My practice is borrowed from the "Crappy Childhood Fairy", Anna Runkle's podcast. I became acquainted with her along with several other presenters during the pandemic. Her Podcasts are insightful and inspiring I expanded on her techniques to include: Fears, Resentments, and Gratitudes. You might visit her Podcast for more information on "Daily Practice". She speaks of CPTSD, and overcoming the impacts on your life, Dysregulation, and getting re-regulated.

The addition of Gratitudes helps me finish the process on a Positive note. Whether large or small, being grateful, for even the air we breathe, for anything remotely available to us. Nothing in life should be taken for granted.......be Grateful. Developing a spirit of gratefulness, leaves very little space in a person's life for Depression to wedge its way in!

Take time to De-velop some newer healthier habits and mindsets, and en-velop them to include them into your pathway to healing from Depression.

Chapter Thirty-Six: DE-TOX

a process or period of time in which one abstains from or rids the body of toxic or unhealthy substances; detoxification.
Toxic
1. poisonous
2. very harmful or unpleasant in a pervasive or insidious way.

We live in a day and time when concern for toxic goes beyond the text book definition above. While there are substances that can be toxic to our bodies, especially when over-consumed, can cause damage to our bodies, there are people that can be "toxic" to our emotional health and psychological well-being.

We all have been around them, the person that has nothing positive to say. The woe is me type. The "world is coming to an end and we're all going to hell with it", type of person.

During the pandemic we have fallen prey to a virus that seemingly had a mind of its own. The death toll seemed exponential at times. But, it isn't through running its course. We've also be apprised by the media of the rise of depression, while blaming it on the pandemic. How many of us have bought into what the media is telling us? The gloom and doom that the media has imposed on us.

Take a moment to look around........how many people in your immediate environment actually had Covid-19. Not to minimize the damage it has caused and the lives that are lost, but we are prone to believe what we are told. Toxic thought processes can feed depression. Buying into what other people tell us about the world we live in and ourselves creates doubt and despair.

Undoubtedly, the Pandemic has changed the way we think about disease and its ability to change our personal habits and lifestyles, but we can counter all of that by creating healthy mindsets and lifestyles.

Protect your mind the way you would protect your body from exposure to disease.

De-tox.........by eliminating toxic people and relationships out of you life.

This may sound extreme but when a person gets a diagnosis of Cancer and it involves a tumor, most would opt to either cut the tumor out or take aggressive actions by means of chemo-therapy or radiation to treat the cancer.

Another way to treat it would be through natural remedies and therapies, exercising, and adopting nutritional habits to improve your quality of life. Many people have stopped smoking when the awareness was created by a label on the side of the package of cigarettes. Warning! We all know what it says......these may cause cancer.

Toxic substances and toxic people can expose us to toxicity. Exposure can change us physiologically and psychologically.

The answer may be the same for the psyche.....eliminate those toxic people out of our lives, or at least limit your exposure to them.

If you are seeking a healing from depression, it might require that you DETOX.

I've suggested in other chapters that you take an inventory or investigate. Ask yourself the tough questions? If you truly desire to rid your life of depression, you may have to be prepared to eliminate Toxic people and substances that prevent you from healing properly.

We are commanded to love others, as ourselves. But we are commanded to love God first. God says to guard your heart and your mind.

Our bodies are a temple. That includes our mind, body and spirit.

A temple is a building devoted to the worship and regarded as a dwelling place.

1 Corinthians 6:19-20 (ESV), he asks, "Or do you not know that your body is a temple of the Holy Spirit within you, whom you have from God? You are not your own, for you were bought with a price. So glorify God in your body."

Romans 12:2 Do not conform to the pattern of this world, but be transformed by the renewing of your mind. Then you will be able to test and approve what God's will is—his good, pleasing and perfect will.

I'm suggesting we protect our mind, body, and spirit from what we "take in". and replace it with life giving scripture and friends, family, and associations, that support our healthy recovery from Depression.

Take the DE-out and detox your life, to move toward a healing from Depression!

Chapter Thirty-Seven: DE-VOTE

1) giving all or a large part of a person's time or resources.
2) invoke or pronounce a curse upon.
Similar: allocate, assign, alot, commit, give, afford, designate, dedicate

When dealing with a decline in health, whether mental or physical, a person often needs to allocate more time to the research and treatment of the disease than usual. Devotion to your own healing takes energy as well as time and financial resources.

I recently made a commitment to write this book, which necessarily meant I had to "set aside" and devote time for writing. A time for daily devotional is common among many religious practices. I devote time in my day for exercise, sleeping, and eating. We all need to set aside or allocate time in our day for healthy practices, mind, body, and spirit. I believe much of what brings on disease, whether it be physical or mental disease, is a lack of balance in our daily living. In order to prevent disease, we must *devote* our time, efforts, resources, and monies, to the establishment of healthy practices and purchases.

For example, it is well-established in medical journals high-fat, high cholesterol eating greatly impacts cardiovascular disease. But so does a lack of exercise or activity.

Devoting time to researching and shopping for healthy foods takes intentional practice. This is difficult to write, knowing we just celebrated a Thanksgiving feast and generally consume on average twice the food we would normally eat in one setting! But it's not a general habit to do so. Healthy habits take time and *devotion*. The treatment of depression is going to take a commitment, or devotion, to certain health practices which may help lessen and ultimately resolve the depression.

One of the symptoms of depression is sleeping more than usual. We live in a sleep deprived society. It is thought the average amount of sleep to maintain health is 6-8 hours a night. Chronic sleep deprivation can lead to depression, often manifested in cloudy thinking, chronic fatigue, and low work production. This can most easily be remedied by turning the T.V. off and getting to bed an hour earlier, as many of us must arise early in the mornings to get to jobs.

I decided to give up a career in teaching and changed careers, so I would have more flexibility in my sleep schedule. Real estate allows me to set my own hours, but it is also a commission-based field, so the change brings different stressors. It really boils down to balancing your time and energies, and devoting time to those things which support a healthy lifestyle. Some other suggestions to devoting your time and resources to healthier habits are:

1) Eat foods low in simple sugar to avoid mood swings and weight gain. Eat foods high in brain nutrients like Omega oils, Choline, and Inositol. It can't hurt to take a supplemental multi-vitamin and mineral, and there are many high-quality products on the market.
2) Exercise daily, preferably some form of aerobic exercise which elevates blood oxygen levels and is heart healthy.
3) Get adequate sleep
4) Adopt a spirit of Gratitude. It's really difficult to be depressed when you are grateful, and joyful.
5) Listen to music that is positive and uplifting.

The JOY of the LORD is my strength. I signed up for daily emails sent to me of positive affirmations and lessons in HOPE.I wake up to a positive podcast every morning! As I am recently divorced and live alone, I don't have to give consideration to my devotionals times and a spouse. I'm devoted to doing everything in my power to bring about a healing from depression and helping others realize a healing is within reach! I still have my down moments, or periods, but over-all, being devoted to healthy practices – mind, body, and spirit – and taking a holistic approach to combating depression has created a more positive mind-set!

This is my quote for today: "Very little is needed to make a happy life." – Marcus Aurelius

Take the DE- out of Devote and Vote for a positive, more healthy you!

Chapter Thirty-Eight: DE-VIL

1) the personification of evil as it is conceived in various cultures and religious traditions.
2) someone or something evil, hurtful or wicked. In many religions, the major personified spirit of evil, ruler of Hell, and foe of God.
Similar: evil spirit, demon, fiend, imp, bogie, ghost, specter, beast, monster, savage, demon, fiend, villain

Today, this very day, my hope is we can change the depression you may be experiencing by taking the De- out and pressing on, taking the De- out and changing the Devil to good. De-vil – take the veil off and turn the situation from evil to good.

Many of you can relate to the concept of good and evil being represented by an angel resting on one shoulder and a devil resting on the other, vying for your attentions when in a questionable circumstance. The first definition describes this personification of evil. The devil can present itself in what others do to you to harm you. I found this to be true with narcissists. This year, while going through a divorce, I identified a quality in my personality which attracts narcissistic men. Then I dug a little de-eper to identify the source. I realized I was raised by a narcissistic father. I delved in deep to dig out those angry roots and gain perspective to prevent myself from falling for the devilish ways of a narcissist again.

We are going to encounter evil in life. It's in the world. It's in people, places, and things. We are also instructed to "be in the world, but not of the world" *(John 17: 14-16)*. God has given us the out from Evil. Raise the "veil." Be in the world, but not of it. We don't have to be a part of the world values which tends to suck us into the worldliness. We can remain set apart from the wickedness of the cosmos as we seek to live a holy, righteous life. Living a righteous life is the ultimate source of happiness. When we don't give in to the worldly standards, we can thrive as happy people.

Psalms 38:4 gives an account of David in woe for his iniquities. "For my iniquities have gone over my head, like the waves of a flood. As a heavy burden they weigh too much for me."

Doesn't this describe depression? It's heaviness is too much for us to bear. Further, David says, "I am bent over and greatly bowed down. I go about mourning all day long." He describes his enemies as "they repay evil for good, they attack and try to kill me."

But wait, he finishes on an upward note, "Do not abandon me, O Lord, O my God, do not be far from me. Make haste to help me, O Lord my salvation." We need to follow David's lead on escaping that mindset, when the enemy of depression pursues us. There is a new day ahead. Psalms 40, "I waited patiently....he heard my cry!" Verse 2, "He brought me up out of a horrible pit (of tumult and destruction), out of the miry clay and he set my feet upon a rock, steadying my footsteps and establishing my path." Speaking positive words of affirmation is biblical! Verse 5, "if I would declare and speak of wonders, they would be too many to count!" Verse 17, "you are my help and my rescuer, do not Delay!"

Every morning I receive an email podcast from Pastor Rick Warren of Saddleback church in California. I thought I would share this one about Happiness.

Pastor Rick describes the four most common "kill-joys" in life as

1) pain

2) pressure

3) people and

4) Problems.

These are the four most common sources of unhappiness.

Happiness is not something you look for, it's something you create. It's a choice. "When and then" thinking is a happiness killer! *When* this happens, *then* I will be happy. One of the happiest books in the bible was written by Paul when he was in the most dismal of circumstances in jail and prison, Philippians.

Paul's example of the principle of happiness, "everything that has happened to me is going to be used for good. Whatever happens conduct yourselves in a manner worthy of the joy of Christ."

I can be happy.

I can be happy.

I can be happy.

When I choose to remember, God can bring good from any situation. *Romans 8:28*WE KNOW: In all things that happen, God works for the Good, to those called according to his purpose. You have to go through a test, to have a testimony. David exclaimed, "I *will* praise the Lord, no matter what happens" Psalms 34:1 The will is our own. We can will ourselves into action and a changed perspective. How do you consistently make the decision to praise, rather than pontificate (Complain).I suggest you choose to look at every situation from outside yourself, to the "bigger picture," from God's perspective; looking past the pain, the pressure, the people, and the problem. Philippians 1:12Paul says, "*everything* that has happened to me, has helped to spread the good news." Paul says, *everything* can be considered good when viewed in light of God's purpose for our lives and his glorification. How can evil be turned to good?

1) Turn a problem into a challenge and take it on with a passion. Change the mindset, change the approach to the circumstance. Face every situation with Faith, not fear.

2) People: Never let others control your attitude. It is your will, not theirs! Encourage other believers. Bless and be blessed. I used to tell teachers in the hallway at school to "bless and be blessed," rather than "bless them out." Be happy in spite of your environment, or circumstances.

3) What others do doesn't really matter, in every way the message of Christ is shared. I am happy and will continue to be happy. Paul models happiness. He won't let anything steal his happiness. *Philippians 1:28*, be constant and fearless, as it is a sign of their destruction and a clear sign of your deliverance. For me, to live is Christ, and to die is gain. *Philippians 1:21.*

Suggestions to combat evil in this world.

4 types of people:

There are four types of people. Choose who you are going to affiliate and associate with.

1. *Critics* are jealous and like to argue.
2. *Companions* are a small group, so when you are under attack you have encouragers.
3. *Competitors* are those coming from selfish ambition. They will rob your happiness.
4. Challengers are people who really just don't like you; Generally, gossipers.

Focuses

- Worship instead of Worry.
- Pray instead of Pontificate (complain).
- Faith instead of Fear.
- Focus on Purpose, not the Problem.
- Do Good. The Devil can't win when we take the devilish deeds of others, and profess
- God will turn it to good!

Let's take the De-out of Devil, and let GOD turn evil into Good in our lives.

Chapter Thirty-Nine: DE-VOID

entirely lacking or free from.
"Lisa kept her voice devoid of emotion"
Similar: lacking, without, free from/of, empty of, vacant of, void of, bare of

There is a condition in Depression described as affect. The underlying experience of feeling, emotion or mood. Emotions are powerful expressions of our states of mind. We feel a wide variety of emotions consciously, subconsciously and unconsciously. Emotions come and go. They may be fleeting or last for hours. The experiences that we have in our daily lives certainly affect our emotions. Our emotions have a solid impact on our relationships and interactions with others. At various times, we feel that we have more control over our emotions than at other times.

Depression is a game changer when it comes to emotions and mood. There are days when a person is Devoid of feeling..... This is usually described as Clinical Depression. Absent of feeling, absent of thought, or reason why a person feels that way. Totally VOID.

Many times, people will try to fill that space, that VOID with things, busyness, additions, material wealth, and many other things......you may fill that blank here......_____.

We all do it.....yes even those of us without depression attempt to fill the emptiness. A VOID i s defined as being empty. VOID of emotions is an absence of expression.

This planet was at one time void of light and life........then GOD said, "Let there be Light." Let's use that parallel to describe what to do if your are feeling the VOID that Depression can create. GOD has not intended for us to feel this way. It's a spiritual VOID that only he can fill. We were created in his image......his likeness. I believe we were created to fill the VOID of loneliness. GOD was alone when created the Earth, the animals and man, then woman.

We are essentially his family while here on earth fulfilling a purpose, to glorify him with everything we do. Genesis 1......and GOD said It was GOOD! He is speaking of his creation....... God's creation filled a VOID....... He is the only one that can fill the VOID in our lives, if you are struggling with Depression, start by identifying the place in your spirit that is wounded, void, or lacking, and fill it with his mercy, grace, and forgiveness. Be comforted by his presence. Today and every day. The following scriptures remind us that GOD is here to fill the VOID!

Exodus 34: 6 The GOD of compassion and mercy! I am slow to anger and FILLED with unfailing love and faithfulness. He was encouraging MOSES in the wilderness.

Psalm 81:10 For it was I, the Lord your GOD who rescued, you from the land of Egypt. Open your mouth side, and I will FILL it with good things".

He fills my life with good things, My youth is renewed like the eagle! When the temptation to fill your life with things, or you time with busy-ness, stop to consider what it is that you are really needing. Many people suffer losses in our lives. Loss of job, loss of friends or loss of family members, loss to death, loss of reputation.......it goes on and on. Losses can leave a huge void or space in our daily lives, and our psyche.

Many fill the VOID with substances, or things that only contribute to a greater problem. Filling a spiritual VOID, can only be accomplished when we are aware of the issues, acknowledge our need for help, and commit to healing or filling the VOID with Godliness. GOD's word, the Holy Bible, is the instruction guide for life. I would like to share the scriptures that surfaced when I used VOID as my guide to research.

John 10: 9-10 I am the Door, anyone who enters through Me will be saved and go in and out and find pasture (spiritual security). The thief comes only in order to steal and kill and destroy, I came that they may have and enjoy life, and have it in abundance.

Job 15:31 I am the Lord your God, who brought you up out of the land of Egypt. Open your mouth wide, and I will **fill** it.

I love metaphors, and the Bible is full of them. Emptiness and loneliness are wake-up calls to go to God, who is the only One who can turn emptiness into fullness, and fill us with His fullness and blessing, even if everything around us remains in emptiness.

In Isaiah, 41:10 God says, "Fear not, for I am with you, Be not dismayed (Depressed), for I am your GOD. I will strengthen you; yes, I will help you, I will uphold you with My righteous.

Music can fill a void...... Do you have a favorite Song that lifts your spirits? In addition, you can use a favorite "Psalms" to lift you spirit. It can also be used to glorify as praise and worship. There is an abundance of beautiful music, but the truly good praise and worship ministers to the VOID you may be feeling. It help my heart to be happy. It 's like a spiritual medication, music can reach deep into your spiritual, mind and body.

I am a published songwriter with BMI. You may You tube, Soldiers Prayer, Collin Raye, which I wrote in 2007. "Deep in the heart of a war, He hears a Soldier's Prayer." Deep in your state of VOID, loneliness, or emptiness, you can be filled with JOY. The JOY of the LORD is my strength. *Nehemiah 8:10*

How can I be filled with God's Word?

4 Easy Ways to Fill Your Home (and your heart) With God's Word

1. Play worship music. Grab your favorite worship CD, DVD, or You-Tube playlist and fill your home with worship!
2. Framed Bible Verse Printables. ... I love refrigeration magnets!
3. Audio Bible Apps. ... Two that I highly recommend
4. Make Memory Verse Cards.

If GOD had ever intended for us to live life in a VOID, or VOID of emotion, he would have never provided us with the glorious creation that we enjoy on planet earth. GOD wants to fill our hearts in the spaces that become VOID (for whatever reasons), just as he filled the planet and brought forth life, GOD can bring life and fill any VOID, that you may be experiencing!

Take the DE- out of Devoid, and let GOD fill you with his JOY and give you the abundant life he promises us. I come to give you life and give it more abundantly.

John 10: 10.

Chapter Forty: DE-PART

leave, especially in order to start a journey.
"they departed for Germany"
Similar: leave, withdraw, absent oneself

deviate from (an accepted, prescribed, or traditional course of action).
"he departed from the precedent set by many"
Similar: deviate, diverge, digress

This chapter ghosted me for weeks. I wasn't sure what I was supposed to do with it. I believe it was the Holy Spirit "nagging" at my heart to include this as a final chapter, though it is out of the alpha sequencing before it.

There is a scripture that I grew up being "bible" thumped with. Seemingly everytime I committed some form of cardinal "sin" or as my mother put it, "rebelled", she would remind me of my upbringing, and the "we didn't raise you like that" was used to remind me or get me back in line. This is somewhat humorous to me today, but also serious. The scripture I'm referring to is: "Train (or raise) up a child in the way he should go and he will not DE-PART from it." Proverbs 22:6.........

But what exactly does that mean? And how should a parent or community "raise up a child"?

I was fortunate, in a lot of respects, to be raised in a 2-parent, Judeo-Christian family environment. Though my father was military and absent many years of my youth, at least what I recall from 5-years to 13 years of age. He was deployed on occasion for overseas missions and assignments. Just before retirement he was utilized as an Army recruiter and traveled throughout the week and only home on weekends. The bulk of my Pre-adolescent teaching and training rested on my mother. Any she was a "Godly-woman", often citing scripture to reinforce her discipline, whether manual or verbal. "Spare the rod spoil the child" philosophy was common in our household. Though I'm also not sure it was intended the way it was used either.

I'd like to present a little different perspective to this philosophy of "Raise up a Child". Given that the 10-commandments are usually the "Laws" to be abided by Christian standards, Let's reflect on those. But let's also reflect on the Beatitudes mentioned in a previous chapter and Matthew 5. I will attempt to combine the trains of thought and factor in where does all of this play out for the individual, the "fearfully and wonderfully made" individual spoken of in Psalms 139:14.

As I mentioned some parents or authorities will use scripture, as a means other than its intended purpose. Though they may be "well-meaning", their actions are that of authoritarian, controlling, blaming, and/or shaming, an individual into compliance.

I truly believe a life lived under an Oppressive, Suppressive, or Repressive spirit, can lead to a Depressed Spirit. Those actions aforementioned can limit one's potential in a way adverse to their true ordained purpose and calling in life.

For instance, many times parents will chose the profession that "they think" is appropriate for their child should and support them financially through college to enable them to succeed.

If it is not in that individuals personality, academic make-up or true desire and passion, it can set them up for much frustration and failure. This can all feed into Depression. So, if a child continually misses the mark, they will feel like they have disappointed the parent and become a "failure". Some parent s will fault the child or young adultby commenting, "I raised you better than that", a form of shaming.

De-parting from the norm may be necessary for that individual to truly honor the uniqueness described as "fearfully and wonderfully made". Though it might be view as rebellion, it is truly the mark of God-given individuality. Only one can decide for themselves what their true calling in life is.

I struggled with this for years. I was a strong athlete and academic, so I got a lot of attention from my father, who had "bragging rights" to my performances.

I later determined as an adult, this was not such a healthy relationship and is common with a narcissistic or authoritative parenting approach. That of, owning or claiming credit for their child's successes, as it brings attention to the parent's capabilities.

You often see this at sporting events, where parents are "Side-line coaches"or enthusiast. This can often create conflicting self-image/self-esteem issues for a child or young adult, when attempting to separate their identity from that of the parent.

Let's use the concept of DE-part here. Even if a child or young adult is raised to respect their parents or authority figures, at some point in order to develop their own sense of self, they would have to own their own performances and learn to appreciate their own individuality, even if genetically predisposed to that trait, albeit, athleticism, academics, musicality, as you see the list goes on.

If a child is shamed, by the use of scripture to control or confine them, could you see how it would create identity issues, and lower their self-esteem.

But, if it is use appropriately, as training is a form of guiding and mentoring, and less into submissive behavior, the child or young adult can develop with a greater sense of self-worth. If you struggle in these areas, I really do understand. I've learned to claim God's grace over those parenting styles and forgive them "for they know not what they do". much of the time. Also, in my parenting attempts, I try not to duplicate that type of parenting style.

Let's consider when an individual is allowed to be an independent-thinker, and use the scripture as a reference point and guideline to check behavior.

I consider 1 Corinthians 13 as a great guide to "raise up a child". Loving them and meeting them where they are. Embracing their individuality while attempting to guide them into strong decision-making skills guided by conscience, values and morale beliefs.

What would this look like? I reference the BEATITUDES. I believe this type of training up a child would create a more adaptable, conscientious human. The traits and qualities of someone who blends into society with a humble helpful heart. Imagine the world we would live in, if this was more the style of parenting. We would all embrace the PART we could play in humanity and bringing forth peace and harmony. Sounds impossible? But God the creator made a world like that "in the beginning". and if we pattern our lives in Christ-like fashion, we too can return to this form of worldly conscious. 1 Corinthians 13, describes the kind of LOVE. What the world needs now is this kind of LOVE.

So let's go ahead, De-PART from this thinking and do our PART, to create a better world. Take time to read the chapter, DE-SERVE again.

Take the DE- out of DE-PART, and own your individuality the way GOD intended.

De-CLARE war on DE-Pression, by taking the DE- out and PRESSing on. Bless and be BLESSED, written with love and humility, JANINE

The Author: Janine Amanda Alexander

The conceptualizing and writing of this book came as the by-product of Janine's personal journey through years in the "wilderness". Her first acknowledgment of having Depression came when she was a classroom teacher, teaching High School Health, Biology and Physical Science.

She is a former competitive athlete as a high school track and basketball athlete, collegiate basketball player, and while eventually competing in international distance triathlons. She was ranked in the top 10 nationally in her age-group at 28 years old, and continued to compete in sprint distance up until she was in her 50's. Janine obtained a B.S.E. in Secondary Education, minors in Physical Education and Biology. Then proceeded to Florida State University, to obtain an M.S. in Exercise Physiology.

Janine is the mother of three adult children and consider them her highest achievement in life....as they are all married and have pursued their respective careers after successfully completing college. Her eldest Daughter, Amanda, is a licensed counseling psychologist with certifications in Sports Psychology.

Amidst all of this, Janine battled with Clinical Depression. She considers herself a "high-achiever", but relates how experiencing Depression impacted all areas of her life. The purpose of this book is to encourage others to ask themselves the tough questions, seek treatment, and explore the spiritual component to Depression. Keep in mind that Janine is not a licensed health care professional and does not intend for this book to substitute for seeking diagnosis, treatment, counseling, or any other form of remedy that an individual has at their disposal or discretion.

Janine believes that if you explore the "root" cause of your personal experience with Depression, many of the chapters in this book will help, en"lighten" you and assist in bringing you out of the darkness that Depression is describes as being; a dark emotion. To stay in line with Janine's original concept of using DE- words, she encourages you to find some of your own, DE- words and write your own chapter on your way to your healing process. Together, we can DE-clare war on Depression which is identified as a "Mental Health" disorder and take a proactive position in our own healing process.

Janine would like to acknowledge those who have encouraged her writings, as mentors that influenced her daily journey by and through their books and Podcasts. They are considered authorities in their respective fields, and not identified in any particular order.

Dr. Les Carter, PhD Psychologist (When Pleasing You is Killing Me) ,
Dr. Ramani Durvasula, PhD Psychologist (Don't You Know Who I Am?)
Dr. Carolyn Leaf, Cognitive Neuroscientist (Switch on Your Brain)
Dr. Brene Brown, Sociology Professor (Braving the Wilderness),
Evangelist and author Joyce Meyer (Battlefield of the Mind)
Pastor and Author Rick Warren (Purpose Driven Life).

Janine would also like to acknowledge the years her personal therapists, Glenda Bates, LMHC, MS, has maintained a high degree of engagement and professionalism, while rendering treatments and modalities, such as ART (Accelerated Resolution Therapy), and Dr. Janice Christenson, EMDR (Eye Movement Desensitization Resolution), for PTSD and Depression.

Janine utilized Joyce Meyer's, "The Everyday Life Bible" to guide her scriptural references, and various online sources, to compare different translations that are cited throughout her manuscript. Stay Hopeful.

From the Everyday Life Bible, Philippians is a book full of principles for living victoriously; a book of great JOY!

Philippians 3: 13-14 Paul says, [13]" I do not consider that I have made it may own yet (he hasn't succeeded yet), but one thing I do.....forgetting what lies behind and reaching forward to what lies ahead. [14] I **press on** toward the goal to win the heavenly prize of the upward call of God in Christ Jesus.

Ecclesiates 9:11 "The race is not always to the swift, nor the battle to the strong, but to the one who holds out. ...Never give up. First, stay focused, and secondly, we must PRESS ON!"

As a work of love and potential healing, JANINE